Elisabeth & Martin Boesch

74   De aedibus

Elisabeth & Martin Boesch

Quart Verlag Luzern

Elisabeth & Martin Boesch
74. Band der Reihe De aedibus / Volume 74 of the series De aedibus

Herausgeber / Edited by: Heinz Wirz, Luzern
Konzept / Concept: Elisabeth & Martin Boesch, Zürich; Heinz Wirz
Projektleitung / Project management: Quart Verlag, Antonia Wirz
Textbeitrag von / Article by: Elisabeth & Martin Boesch
Redaktion Textbeitrag / Article editing: Christoph Schläppi, Bern
Objekttexte / Project descriptions: Elisabeth & Martin Boesch
Vorwort / Foreword: Heinz Wirz, Luzern
Textlektorat Deutsch / German text editing: Miriam Seifert-Waibel, Hamburg
Übersetzung aus dem Deutschen / English translation: Benjamin Liebelt, Berlin
Fotos / Photos: Martin Boesch, Zürich; ausser / except: Martin Gasser, Weinfelden
S. / p. 31 (unten rechts / bottom right); Dominique Meienberg, Zürich S. / p. 37 (Mitte / centre);
Fabian Kiepenheuer, Zürich S. / p. 57 (Luftaufnahme / aerial photograph); Nils Krämer, Eckernförde
S. / p. 71 (oben rechts / top right), 86, 88 (Mitte / centre)
Grafische Umsetzung / Graphic Design: Quart Verlag, Antonia Wirz
Lithos: Printeria, Luzern
Druck / Printing: Printer Trento S.R.L., Trento I

© Copyright 2018
Quart Verlag Luzern, Heinz Wirz
Alle Rechte vorbehalten / All rights reserved
ISBN 978-3-03761-006-0

Quart Verlag GmbH
Denkmalstrasse 2, CH-6006 Luzern
books@quart.ch, www.quart.ch

7	De aedibus 74 – Notat
	Heinz Wirz
8	Diverses / Miscellaneous
	Elisabeth & Martin Boesch
16	Um- und Anbau Haus B-T / Conversion and extension of B-T house, Feldmeilen
22	Umbauten in / Conversions in Berlin, Tokio, Hongkong etc.
28	Drei Umbauten / Three conversions, Basel, Lausanne
30	Neuausbau eines Geschäftshauses / New interior work for a commercial building, Zürich
32	Instandsetzung Verwaltungsgebäude / Renovation of an administration building, Niederurnen
34	Umbau und Instandsetzung Amtshaus III / Conversion and renovation of Amtshaus III, Zürich
36	Umbau Werkhof Uraniastrasse / Maintenance depot conversion, Uraniastrasse, Zürich
40	Begegnungszentrum, psychiatrische Klinik, Königsfelden / Meeting centre, Königsfelden Psychiatric Clinic
42	Kindergarten, Mollis
44	Instandsetzung Haus Kind / Renovation, Kind house, Riehen
46	Wohnhaus S-M / S-M residential building, Zürich
48	Gartenhalle, Gartenhaus / Garden hall and summerhouse, Berneck
50	Pavillon Oui!, expo.02, Yverdon-les-Bains
58	Umbau und Erweiterung Musikinsel Kloster Rheinau / Renovation and extension of the Rheinau Monastery
60	Areal Feldbach / Feldbach site, Steckborn
62	Maag-Areal Plus, Zürich
64	Städtebauliche Studie Lagerplatz (Sulzerareal) / Urban development study, Lagerplatz (Sulzerareal), Winterthur
66	Städtebauliche Studie Tour Henri / Urban planning study, Tour Henri, Fribourg
68	Um- und Anbau Villa Rainhof / Conversion and extension, Villa Rainhof, Zürich
76	Instandsetzung, Umbau und Erweiterung Kurtheater / Renovation, conversion and extension, Kurtheater, Baden
80	Instandsetzung und Umbau Kongresshaus/Tonhalle / Renovation and conversion of the Kongresshaus-Tonhalle, Zürich
84	Sanierung Hardbrücke und fünf Aufgänge / Hardbrücke renovation including five staircases, Zürich
90	Werkverzeichnis / List of works
94	Biografien / Biographies

De aedibus 74 – Notat
Heinz Wirz

"The initial situation with respect to a catalogue of requirements is the existing structure and an exact knowledge of its material and immaterial values. The object is regarded with an equal measure of sobriety and empathy." –
"Bringing new and old elements closer together is a difficult path that is almost always preferable to the simpler and often more destructive contrasting of old and new. Combining is harder than separating."

These two fundamental statements in the introductory text by Elisabeth and Martin Boesch are cornerstones of the architectural couple's work. One refers to analysis, the other to action. The text printed in this volume is a small universe of observations, considerations and directions that are constantly in dialogue with their own concrete tasks. The text is like an exciting draft guideline and theory for renovating and restoration tasks. Such an investigation is necessary today more than ever.
The development of towns and their agglomerations is becoming ever denser and the amount of buildings requiring renovation is growing exponentially. Yet the task of restoration, renovation and continued construction is a discipline that is not often consciously appreciated, both in practice and in teaching. We know of only a few well-founded statements and opinions on the subject from architects; the debate mainly focuses on monumental preservation. Publications such as Adolf Krischanitz's 1989 book on the renewal of Vienna's experimental Werkbund settlement remain marginal. In fact since the work of Carlo Scarpa in northern Italy between the 40s and 70s, the first conscious attempts to acquire and deepen knowledge of this specific task were made in Austria in the 1980s – among others by Hermann Czech and Adolf Krischanitz.
This volume presents a contemporary, independent architectural perspective. It is guided by an unlimited curiosity with respect to existing structures. The architects grow into the existing building and its creator's original design. They internalise the task and find solutions from the qualities that already apply in the existing building. In this way, they draw attention to a new, viable culture of renovation, restoration and continued construction, representing an act of launching into a period that will be filled with more renewal than any other before it.

Lucerne, April 2018

Diverses
Elisabeth & Martin Boesch

Miscellaneous
Elisabeth & Martin Boesch

1 «Vernunft ist die Fähigkeit, objektiv zu denken. Die ihr zugrundeliegende emotionale Haltung ist die Demut. Man kann nur objektiv sein und sich seiner Vernunft bedienen, wenn man demütig geworden ist und seine Kindheitsträume von Allwissenheit und Allmacht überwunden hat.» [...] «Da die Fähigkeit, zu lieben davon abhängt, dass unser Narzissmus relativ gering ist, verlangt diese Kunst die Entwicklung von Demut, Objektivität und Vernunft.»
Erich Fromm in *Die Kunst des Liebens*.
2 In Anlehnung an Heinrich Tessenows Text *Empfindsames über das Teilen und Verbinden in Hausbau und dergleichen*. Berlin: Bruno Cassirer Verlag 1916. S. 47 ff.
3 Merksatz für die Studierenden, die nach klassischer Formung zu Architektinnen und Architekten zum ersten Mal mit einem bestehenden Bau konfrontiert sind.
4 Bernhard Hoesli pflegte diese Unterscheidung jeweils im Entwurfskurs des ersten Studienjahres an der ETH Zürich zu machen.

1 "Reason is the ability to think objectively. The emotional attitude upon which it is based is humility. One can only be objective and use one's reason if one has become humble and has overcome one's childhood dreams of omniscience and omnipotence." [...] "Since the ability to love depends on our narcissism being relatively low, this art requires the development of humility, objectivity and reason." Erich Fromm in *The Art of Loving*.
2 Cf. Heinrich Tessenow's text *Empfindsames über das Teilen und Verbinden in Hausbau und dergleichen*. Berlin: Bruno Cassirer Verlag, 1916. p. 47 ff.
3 Note to students who, following their classical training to become architects, are confronted for the first time with an existing building.
4 Bernhard Hoesli maintained this distinction in his Design courses for first-year students at the ETH Zurich.

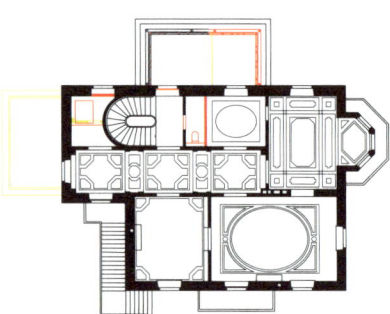

Ob man sich mit bestehenden Gebäuden oder mit ehemaligen Industriearealen befasst, mit dem grösseren oder kleineren Massstab, methodisch bleibt die Herangehensweise trotz aller Unterschiede in der Aufgabenstellung gleich: Ausgangspunkt gegenüber einem Katalog von neuen Bedürfnissen sind der gebaute Bestand und die genaue Kenntnis seiner materiellen und immateriellen Werte. Die Betrachtung des Gegenstandes erfolgt gleichermassen mit kaltem Blick wie mit Empathie. Die Schlüsse, die in diesem Spannungsfeld gezogen werden, variieren. Sie sind, bei allen Gemeinsamkeiten, jedes Mal neu zu erarbeiten – von Fall zu Fall. Ist der eine sozusagen von Entsagung, Demut[1] – welch altertümliche Wörter – geprägt, was bedeutet, dass der Architekt möglichst auf eigenen Ausdruck verzichtet (Eternit-Verwaltungsgebäude), so stellt sich beim anderen die unumgängliche Frage nach dem Ausdruck einer neuen Einheit aus Bestand und Neuem, ausgelöst durch die Forderung nach einer markanten Vergrösserung (Kurtheater Baden). Die Annäherung des Neuen an das Alte ist der schwierigere Weg und fast immer dem einfacheren des letztlich oft destruktiven Kontrastierens von Alt und Neu vorzuziehen. Verbinden ist schwieriger als trennen.[2]

Il lavoro con l'edificio esistente è una disciplina lenta[3]
«Ideen (andere sprechen von Konzepten) fallen – im Gegensatz zu Einfällen[4] – nicht vom Himmel. Oder nur in seltenen Fällen. Die Idee für den Expo-Pavillon, sozusagen der Umbau eines vom Militär erstellten Stegprovisoriums, ist uns derart zugefallen. Eine lange Beschäftigung mit verwandten Fragen, projektierend wie forschend, ging voran. Im Anfang ist das Objekt, das Vorhandene, und danach kommt die Idee: Sie entsteht aus dem Objekt, dem Vorhandenen, heraus und nicht umgekehrt. Das Objekt muss nicht gefallen, aber es wäre unsinnig, Widerstand zu leisten, sich ihm zu widersetzen und ihm nicht ein gewisses Vertrauen entgegenzubringen. Man muss bereit sein, sich auf etwas einzulassen, das ein anderer erdacht hat. Man muss in die Logik des Objektes eindringen, sich einfühlen, sie verstehen, man muss dessen physische Substanz kennen und einer werdenden Projektidee Raum geben, damit sie sich entwickeln kann. Vor und nach dem Eingang der Idee steht das Instrument der Arbeitshypothese; in die Breite schaffen – manchmal tun sich dabei neue Wege auf –, um danach einzuengen und eine Wahl zu begründen. Der Idee folgt die Knochenarbeit, die Verifikation, das Überprüfen und langwierige Umsetzen. Die Baustelle löst eine weitere Planung aus. Mit ihren unzäh-

Whether dealing with existing buildings or former industrial estates, with large or small scales, the approach is methodically the same despite all the differences in the task at hand: The starting point with respect to a catalogue of requirements is the existing structure and an exact knowledge of its material and immaterial values. The object is regarded with an equal measure of sobriety and empathy. The conclusions vary. Despite all the common aspects, they must be newly elaborated each time – from case to case. If one of those cases is characterised by renunciation and humility[1] – what old fashioned words – meaning the architect abstains from his own expression as much as possible (Eternit administration building), the other case poses the inevitable question of the expression of a new unity of existing structures and new elements, caused by the call for a considerable extension (Kurtheater Baden). Bringing new and old elements closer together is the more difficult path that is almost always preferable to the simpler path of contrasting old and new. Combining is harder than separating.[2]

Working on existing buildings is a slow discipline.[3]
Ideas (others speak of concepts) – as opposed to sudden inspiration[4] – do not just fall from the sky. Or only in rare cases. The idea for the Expo pavilion, so to speak the conversion of an improvised jetty, did in fact come to us in that way. But we were prepared, having previously dealt at length with related questions through projects and research.
It all begins with the object, the existing structure, and then the idea follows. It is derived from the already existent object and not the other way around. The object need not be appealing, but it would be absurd to resist it, oppose it and fail to offer it a certain amount of trust. It is essential to be willing to engage oneself in something that another person has conceived. One must enter into the logic of the object, empathize with it, understand it, know its physical substance, and leave scope for a nascent project idea. The instrument of a working hypothesis comes before and after the idea's inception; broad-based working – sometimes thereby finding new paths – before subsequently narrowing down and accounting for a decision. The idea is followed by hard work, verification, checking and the long process of implementation. The building site provokes further planning. Its countless individual cases, unforeseen events, the surprises that are unique to the project, ideally lead to a more focused project (for example the new common room in the Amtshaus III by the

ligen Einzelfällen, mit ihrem Unvorhergesehenen, den ihr eigenen Überraschungen, führt sie im besten Fall zu einer Schärfung des Projektes (Beispiel neuer Pausenraum im Amtshaus III von Stadtbaumeister Gustav Gull, Zürich). Schön, dass man nicht ganz auf sich alleine gestellt ist. Auf viele Fragen hält das Gebäude eine Antwort bereit, weil viele unserer heutigen Fragen nicht anders sind als die von unserem Vorgänger gestellten. Die Halbwertszeit mancher Dinge, Lösungen, Prinzipien und Themen ist um einiges länger als die Tagesaktualität glauben macht. Nur dort, wo neue Fragen gestellt und somit auch noch keine Antworten gegeben sind, müssen wir entwerfen – und es ist, wir lassen unseren Vorgänger uns dabei freundlich über die Schulter schauen. Alles andere entwirft sich von selbst. Entwerfen im Bestand hat einen Rahmen: die Charta von Venedig von 1964. Ihre Grundsätze wie die Forderung nach Substanzerhalt oder nach Reversibilität und Ablesbarkeit eines Eingriffes sind gültig. Doch sie bedürfen von Fall zu Fall der kritischen Befragung. Wie viele Treppenaugen und Hofräume und Baukörper wurden und werden unter dem Vorwand des Substanzerhaltes, der Reversibilität und der Ablesbarkeit für einen Aufzug geopfert? Blind-gehorsam die Regeln befolgend, werden dabei meist alle drei Gebote grob verletzt. Raum wird nicht als Substanz anerkannt. Die Arbeit mit bestehenden Bauten ist nie konfliktfrei, überall lauern Fallen und Widersprüche. Daraus bezieht sie ihre Spannung und Intensität. Ihre Dauer dient der Reifung des Projektes. Die Arbeit mit bestehenden Gebäuden ist eine langsame Disziplin.

Durch Zusammenarbeit zur *solution élégante*[5]
Das 1863 vermutlich von dem Architekten Leonhard Zeugheer in spätklassizistischem Stil errichtete herrschaftliche Wohnhaus an der Rämistrasse 66 in Zürich sollte für das Orientalische Seminar und die Abteilung Indologie des Indogermanischen Seminars der Universität Zürich ertüchtigt und um ein «Bücherdepot» erweitert werden. Die letzte denkmalpflegerische Sanierung lag noch nicht weit zurück. Somit umfassten die anstehenden Arbeiten in und an der Villa nur Teilbereiche, kleinere räumliche Klärungen, Retuschen und einen Pausenraum, der durch die Spiegelung der kleinen Veranda über dem Eingang entstand. Die grössten Eingriffe waren die Anpassung der EDV-Installationen und ein Aufzug. Vieles sprach dafür, die Bibliothek, wie im Wettbewerbsprogramm gefordert, auf der Talseite d. h. unter dem Garten anzuordnen. Mehr sprach dafür, sie bergseitig unter der Vorfahrt anzulegen. Der Verstoss, Resultat eines produktiven Ungehorsams aus Not-

municipal architect Builder Gustav Gull). It is good that one is not completely alone in the process. The building provides answers to many questions. Because many of our questions today are no different from those posed by our predecessors. The half-life of some things, solutions, principles and themes is much longer than day-to-day topics might suggest. Only where new questions arise and no answer has yet been provided must we design – and it is better for us to let our predecessor take a friendly look over our shoulders while doing so. Everything else designs itself. Designing on existing structures has a framework, the 1964 Venice Charta. Its principles, such as the call for preserving substance or the reversibility and traceability of measures, apply. But they must be critically questioned from case to case. How many staircase wells, courtyards and volumes have been and continue to be sacrificed for an elevator, on the grounds of preserving the substance, reversibility and traceability? Blindly adhering to the rules often seriously breaches all three instructions. Space is not recognised as substance. Working on existing buildings is never conflict-free, as pitfalls and contradictions lurk everywhere. That is where their tension and intensity stem from. The duration of the design work serves to mature the project. Working on existing buildings is a slow discipline.

Collaboration to achieve a *solution élégante*[5]
The stately, late classicist villa in Rämistrasse 66, Zurich, which was probably built by the architect Leonhard Zeugheer in 1863, needed strengthening and extending to include a "book depot" for the Oriental Seminar and the Department of Indology at the Indo-Germanic Seminar of the University of Zurich. Its last preservation and renovation had been carried out not long before. So the required work on the villa focused only on partial elements, small spatial clarifications, retouching and a common room created by mirroring the small veranda above the entrance. The largest measure was adapting the IT installations and an elevator. There were many arguments in favour of aligning the library on the valley side, i.e. beneath the garden, as required by the competition programme. But there were even more reasons to place it on the hill side, beneath the drive. This programme transgression, the result of a necessary breach of the rules, reaped rewards since it allowed the garden outside to remain authentic, while...
A concrete wall with multiple folds surrounds the library room. On the hill side, it resists the pressure of the slope and plays about the roots of two

[5] Mehr dazu im Aufsatz von Bruno Reichlin *Das Nützliche ist nicht das Schöne*. In: Daidalos Nr. 64 1997. S. 32–54

[5] Bruno Reichlin discusses this aspect further in his essay *Solution élégante – l'utile n'est pas le beau*. In: *Le Corbusier – unde encyclopédie*. Ouvrage publié à l'occasion de l'exposition *L'aventure Le Corbusier*. Paris 1987

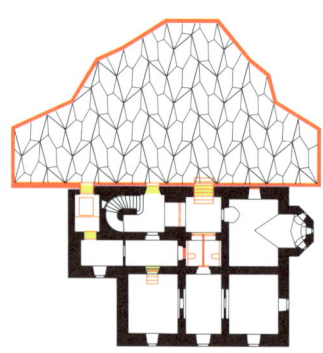

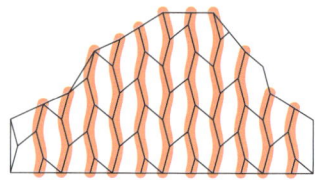

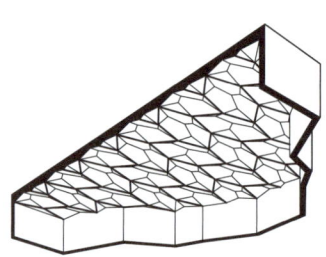

wendigkeit, wurde honoriert. Somit blieb im Äussern der Garten glaubwürdig und im Innern entwarf sich die geschmeidige Wegführung wie von selbst.
Eine mehrfach geknickte Betonmauer umfasst den Bibliotheksraum. Bergseitig stemmt sie sich gegen den Hangdruck und umspielt die Wurzeln zweier stattlicher Bäume. Die Form dieser Mauer ist eine von vielen ähnlich guten Möglichkeiten. (So wie die Stellung der Stützen im Expo-Pavillon nicht einem einzigen Gesetz, zum Beispiel der Reihung oder einem Raster unterliegt, sondern durch eine Vielzahl von Parametern unterschiedlichster Natur geordnet wird. So zwingend die gebaute Ordnung ist – auch sie ist nur eine von vielen ähnlich guten Möglichkeiten.) Auf der Betonmauer liegt die Decke. Bereits im Wettbewerb hat sie ein Relief und ist ungerichtet. Referenzbild war ein an sich zweidimensionales *walldrawing* von Sol LeWitt, ein skizzenartig suchender Verweis auf die geometrisch-räumliche Behandlung von Flächen, wie sie auch im arabischen und indischen Kulturraum mit unterschiedlichen Prägungen vorkommt. Gemeinsam mit dem Bauingenieur (Walt+Galmarini) und dem Künstler und Mathematiker (Urs B. Roth) werden Form und Statik weiterentwickelt. Sie sind das Resultat des fruchtbaren Zusammen- und Ineinanderwirkens von Fachkompetenz, eine Folge der gegenseitigen und verständigen Einmischung. Der Beitrag jeder Disziplin ist beschreibbar und geht gleichzeitig in einem Ganzen auf.[6] Das künstlerisch-mathematisch präzisierte Deckenrelief lässt sich als komplexe Geometrie mit sich wiederholenden Einheiten, genauer als periodisches Pattern mit gleitgespiegelten Elementen beschreiben. Es erlaubt innerhalb der knappen statischen Höhe die Aufnahme von Vorspannkabeln in gestreckter S-Form. Die technisch machbare, aber aufwendige Bügel- und Netzarmierung wird im Laufe der Diskussion durch eine Nagelarmierung ersetzt. So wird die Decke mit ihrem unsichtbaren Innenleben beispielhaft zur *solution élégante*. Die Relieffelder werden nach einem Farbkonzept lasiert. Verstreut angeordnete Lichtpunkte in der Decke stellen einen Bezug zwischen Innen- und Aussenwelt her. Das Projekt wurde bis und mit Baueingabe bearbeitet.
Wiederum in Zusammenarbeit mit Walt + Galmarini und Urs B. Roth erfahren die fünf neuen Treppenaufgänge zur Hardbrücke in Zürich ihre nötige formliche Schärfung. Die Rampe folgt den Gesetzen der logarithmischen Spirale und vereinigt das gute Trittmass mit der schönen Form. So komplex die Form ist, im Querschnitt auskragend und sich verjüngend, so einfach ist die Schalung, die sich aus einer Vielzahl gleicher, horizontal gelegter Schalungsbrettchen ergibt.

mighty trees. The form of the wall is one of many similarly good possibilities. (Just as the supports for the Expo pavilion are not based on a single law, such as rows or a grid, but are instead ordered by a large number of contrasting parameters: however binding the constructed order may be – it too is only one of many comparable possibilities.) The ceiling rests on the concrete roof. Even for the competition, it already had a relief and was unaligned. The reference image was actually a two-dimensional *wall drawing* by Sol LeWitt, a sketch-like searching reference in the geometric-spatial treatment of surfaces, like those that exist in a wide range of characters in Arab and Indian cultures. The form and statics evolved in collaboration with the civil engineer (Walt + Galmarini) and the artist and mathematician (Urs B. Roth). They are the result of fruitful partnership and integrated interaction between different experts, leading to mutual, understanding intervention. The contribution of each discipline is distinctive and yet merges to form a unity.[6] The artistically and mathematically defined ceiling relief can be described as a complex geometry with recurring units, or more precisely as a periodic pattern with glide-reflected elements. It permits the reception of prestressing cables in a stretched S-shape despite the low static height. During the course of discussions, the technically feasable, but difficult clamp and mesh reinforcement is replaced by nail reinforcement. The ceiling and its invisible internal elements thereby become exemplary as a *solution élégante*. The relief fields are varnished according to a colour concept. Points of light on the ceiling are arranged in a scattered way to create a reference between the interior and exterior world. The project was developed through to planning application.
Another project in collaboration with Walt + Galmarini and Urs B. Roth added the necessary formal sharpness to the five new staircases for Zurich Hardbrücke. The ramp follows the laws of a logarithmic spiral and combines a good stepping height with a beautiful form. Despite the complex form, with its cantilevered and narrowing cross-section is, its mould is simple, resulting from a large number of identical, horizontally laid shutter boards.

Architectural density and the level of detailing
Each project is a unique case. A similar level of detail as the existing structure is often appropriate. Exceptions confirm the rule.
One example is the wall and ceiling treatment in the Villa Rainhof in Zurich. We could have played on the subject of panelling and calico, as well as white plaster on the surfaces, in a contemporary way. This is com-

Architektonische Dichte und Detaillierungsgrad

Jedes Projekt ist ein Fall für sich. Ein ähnlicher Detaillierungsgrad wie beim Bestehenden ist oft angemessen. Ausnahmen bestätigen die Regel.

Ein Beispiel ist die Wand- und Deckenbehandlung in der Villa Rainhof in Zürich. Das Thema Täfer und Calicot bzw. Weissputz für die Oberflächen liesse sich zeitgemäss «reduziert» durchspielen. Man kennt das. Stattdessen haben wir das Wissen um das handwerkliche Machen, das Wissen um die Gründe, weshalb etwas sinnvollerweise so oder anders gemacht wird, zur Anreicherung, zur Erhöhung und Steigerung der *architektonischen Dichte* der zu nackt-kahlen Räume frucht- und nutzbar gemacht. Ein Gewebe überbrückt kleine Risse, die sich ohnehin wieder einstellen werden, verändert Optik und Haptik der Wandoberfläche und schafft Differenz zur Decke. Erstere ist Teil der Wandmasse (aussen Backstein, innen Holzständer mit Backsteinausfachung), die andere ist Teil einer Membran zum Deckenhohlraum (Holzbalkendecke). Das Eckprofil gibt dem schwierigen Zusammentreffen von Wand und Decke Form, Licht und Schatten, dem Tapezierer deckt es den wegen dem Problem des Schrumpfens schwierigen oberen Anfang des wie eine Tapete mit Leim aufgebrachten Gewebes. Folgerichtig ist das Eckprofil eine Einheit aus zwei Teilen: ist Gipsstab an der Decke und Holzstab an der Wand. Wand und Decke sind gleichfarbig. Die Raumwirkung ist «umfassend». Das Täfer gliedert, proportioniert, schützt und entlastet die Wand im unteren Bereich. Es nimmt die Elektroleitungen auf und festigt den neuen inneren Horizont[7] der Räume, deren Proportionen durch das Einziehen von unumgänglichen tiefer gehängten Decken erheblich verändert wurden. Das Täfer dient sowohl der Gestaltung wie den Abhängigkeiten des Machens auf der Baustelle. MDF-Platten unterscheiden sich von der üblicherweise traditionell gefügten und dadurch gezeichneten Konstruktion aus Tannenholz (Bretter oder Rahmen mit Futter) und eröffnen andere Möglichkeiten des Ausdrucks. Die mit Ölfarbe und Pinselauftrag behandelten Platten werden mittels vertiefter Zeichnungen – mit CNC-gesteuerten Maschinen in die Oberfläche eingefrästen Gravuren – der flachen Banalität entzogen. Die acht Motive für die acht mit Täfer versehenen Seminar- und Büroräume sind hergeleitet aus im Haus zurückgelassenen Herbarien und sind damit der Geschichte, dem Inhalt und dem Ort des Hauses verbunden. Der kleine Reichtum des Fügens von Teilen – ein Relief auf unterschiedlichen Ebenen und mit unterschiedlichen Aufgaben – verbindet ganz beiläufig die neuen Täfer mit den bestehenden oder die mit Kopien ergänzten Holzeinfassungen der Fenster und mit den Holzgittern vor den Radiatoren.

mon. Instead, we used our knowledge of craftsmanship, knowledge of the reasons why something is necessarily done that way and not in a different way, to enrich, heighten and increase the architectural density of the naked, raw rooms and create something fruitful and useful. A tissue bridges small cracks, which will in any case reappear, thereby changing the visual and haptic qualities of the wall surface, and creating a contrast with the ceiling. The former is part of the wall mass (outer brick, inner timber framework with brick infilling), while the latter is part of the membrane towards the ceiling cavity (wooden beam ceiling). The corner profile gives the difficult joint between the wall and ceiling form, light and shadow. For paperhangers, it solves the difficult problem of shrinkage when attaching the textile, which is pasted like wallpaper from the top. So the corner profile is a unit made of two parts, a plaster profile on the ceiling and a wooden profile on the wall. The wall and ceiling have the same colour. The spatial effect is "enveloping". The panelling structures, proportionates, protects and relieves the wall in the lower section. It holds the power cabling and fixes the new inner horizon[7] of rooms, with proportions that are considerably changed due to the inevitably lowered ceilings. The panelling serves both the design and the technical dependencies on the construction site. MDF boards distinguish themselves from the normally used, traditionally joined, patterned fir construction (boards or frames with lining) and thereby provide new expressive possibilities. The boards, which are brush-coated with oil paints, have sunken drawings – milled engravings using CNC-controlled machines – that remove any flat banality. The eight motifs for the eight seminar and office rooms with decorative panels are derived from the herbariums left behind in the building and are thereby connected to its history, the content and the location. The small luxury of joining parts – a relief on different levels and with varying tasks – casually connects the new panels to the existing timber surrounds for the windows or their new supplementary copies, as well as the wooden slats in front of the radiators. The form and construction for all of the additionally required doors is dictated by the existing frames and stemmed doors from 1867 on the top floor, as well as the doorframes and smooth doors from the 1950s on the ground and first floors. The profiled, rounded 1950s doorframes are gratefully accepted as guidance for the profiling of the new wooden showcases and the fire-resistant glazings between the halls and the (emergency) staircase. One refers to the other, as everything is unabashedly traditional and yet contemporary.

---

6 Andernorts ist es die Zusammenarbeit zum Beispiel mit dem Bauphysiker oder dem Planer der Haustechnik, welche zum schlüssigen Resultat führt.

7 Wir beziehen uns hier auf Hannie van Eycks Begriff des *inner horizon*.

6 Elsewhere, it is collaboration with construction physicists or building technology planners that leads to a coherent result.

7 We refer here to Hannie van Eyck's understanding of the term *inner horizon*.

Mit den vorhandenen Zargen und gestemmten Türen von 1867 im Dachgeschoss bzw. den Türzargen und glatten Türen aus den 1950er-Jahren im Erd- und Obergeschoss sind Form und Konstruktion für die je zu ergänzenden Türen gegeben. Für die Profilierung der neuen hölzernen Vitrinengehäuse, desgleichen für die Brandabschlüsse aus Glas und Holz zwischen Hallen und Treppenraum (Fluchttreppe), werden die stark profilierten und gerundeten Zargen der 1950er-Jahre als Anleitung dankbar angenommen. Das eine verweist auf das andere. Und das Ganze ist so ungehemmt traditionell wie zeitgenössisch.

Welcher Härtegrad?
Unsere Aufmerksamkeit beim Entwurf gilt oft einer Eigenschaft von Bauten, die wir als «Härtegrad» bezeichnen. Dieser ist von Projekt zu Projekt neu zu definieren. Oft erweist es sich als sinnvoll, den Härtegrad einer Hinzufügung demjenigen des Bestehenden anzugleichen.
Beispiel eins: Ertüchtigung des Amtshauses III von Gustav Gull. Zu Beginn der Planung 1997 entsprach der Brandschutz teils dem Stand von 1914. Die bei Sanierungen gängigen Detaillösungen hätten vielerorts zu Verfälschungen geführt (z. B. Aufdoppelungen und deren Folgen), die Probleme mussten konzeptionell angegangen werden. In enger Zusammenarbeit mit Feuerpolizei und Denkmalpflege wurde eine Strategie erarbeitet, welche es erlaubte, die Korridore mit Türen und Wandschmuck aus Tanne und einfachsten Oberlichtern integral zu erhalten. Dafür waren an einigen Stellen Brandschutztüren einzuführen. Diese sind üblicherweise aus Stahl und bedürfen angesichts der verlangten Grösse eines Kämpfers. Harte Metalle wie Messing oder Eisen hatte Gull nur dort eingesetzt, wo sie auch wirklich nötig waren bei Türdrückern, Beschlägen und Fenstergittern. Diese Regel und Gewichtung bestimmte den Charakter mit und war zu respektieren. Als wir bei der ersten Begehung mit den zuständigen Ämtern anmeldeten, dass diese Türen aus Holz sein müssten, wurde unser Ansinnen belächelt. Die 1999 nach zweijähriger Vorlaufzeit eingebauten Brandabschnitttüren sind reine Holzkonstruktionen und haben keine Kämpfer, dafür ein EU-Gutachten. Die selbsttragenden Türrahmen erhielten eine Profilierung.
Beispiel zwei: der Anbau der Villa Rainhof. Der Hauptbau hat Aussenmauern aus Backstein und Innenwände aus Holzständern mit Backsteinausfachung, seine Tür- und Fenstergewände sind aus Sandsteinelementen zusammengesetzt, die oberen Geschosse haben Holzbalkendecken. Der Anbau ist dem Hauptbau durch seine Grösse und Bedeutung hierarchisch untergeordnet. Er ist nicht monolithisch, sondern aus

What degree of hardness?
When designing, we often focus our attention on an aspect of buildings that we call the "degree of hardness". It is redefined with each new project. Often it is sensible to adapt an extension's "degree of hardness" to that of the existing building.
Example one: strengthening the Amtshaus III by Gustav Gull. At the start of planning in 1997, some of the fire protection measures only fulfilled the regulations of 1914. The detailed solutions commonly used for renovations would have led to adulteration in many places (for instance doubling and its consequences), so the problems had to be tackled conceptually. In close collaboration with the fire protection and monumental preservation authorities, a strategy was developed that permitted the corridors, with their fir-wood doors and wall decorations, as well as the simplest skylights, to be retained as integral parts. As a result, fire-resistant doors had to be installed in a number of places. They are usually made of steel and glass and require transoms due to their weight. But Gull had only used hard metals such as brass or iron where absolutely necessary, for door handles, fittings and window gratings. This rule and weighting had an influence on the building's character and had to be respected. During the first inspection, when we told the relevant authorities that these doors had to be made of wood and glass, our request was scoffed at. And yet in 1999, the fire-resistant doors installed after a development period of two years were purely wooden constructions and had no transoms, but they did have an EU certificate. The self-supporting doorframes were profiled.
Example two: extension to the Villa Rainhof. The main building has exterior walls made of brick and interior walls consisting of wooden pillars with brick infilling, while the door and window linings are made of sandstone elements. The upper storeys have wooden joist ceilings. The extension is hierarchically subordinate to the main building due to its size and significance. It is not monolithic and instead consists of prefabricated concrete elements – supports and beams. Despite the differences, both in terms of structure and expression, the extension's configuration creates a proximity to the existing building. Both are similarly "soft". The same extension made of in-situ concrete would have involved significantly less intensive planning and implementation work, but would also have been too self-referential and too hard.

Interior spaces
These are fragile and the first victims of change, often after only a very short time. And yet they are

Quart
Architektur

www.quart.ch

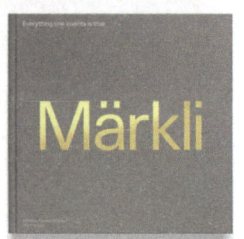

Peter Märkli – Everything one invents is true

Peter Märkli zählt seit den frühen 1980er-Jahren zweifellos zu den markantesten Deutschschweizer Architekten der ersten Stunde. Seine einprägsamen Bauten lassen sich jedoch nicht leicht in das Schema dieser Architekturbewegung einordnen. Zu sehr sind die einzelnen Bauwerke intensiv bearbeitete Individuen, die einer fortdauernden Bewegung des Suchens folgen. Immer eröffnen sie eigenständig und eindringlich Verbindungen der Geschichte der Architektur mit dem Impetus einer zeitüber-dauernden Gültigkeit.
Im vorliegenden Band sind 17 Bauten der letzten 15 Jahre mit Texten, Plänen und Abbildungen ausführlich dargestellt.

Since the early 1980s, Peter Märkli has been one of the most striking protagonists of German Swiss architecture from the earliest period of its emergence. However his impressive buildings cannot be easily classified in the scheme of this architectural movement, since the individual buildings are intensely developed individuals that follow the continuous movement of seeking. They always open up connections with the history of architecture in an independent, powerful way and express the impetus of timeless validity.
This volume presents 17 buildings in detail from the last 15 years with texts, plans and images.

Herausgegeben von / Edited by Pamela Johnston
Textbeiträge / Essays by: Florian Beigel & Philip Christou, Pamela Johnston, Peter Märkli, Elena Markus, Franz Wanner, Ellis Woodman

240 Seiten / pages, 29 × 29 cm
178 Abbildungen / illustrations, 101 Skizzen / sketches, 75 Pläne / plans
Hardcover, fadengeheftet / Hardcover, thread-stitched

English ISBN 978-3-03761-138-8: eingelegtes Booklet mit Essays in Deutsch / with an enclosed booklet containing the essays in German.

English ISBN 978-3-03761-139-5: eingelegtes Booklet mit den Projekttexten in Japanisch / with an enclosed booklet containing the project texts in Japanese.

CHF 138.– / EUR 126.–

Wohnsiedlung / Housing estate Im Gut, Zürich, 2012–2014

Schule / School Im Birch, Zürich-Oerlikon, 2004

Gion A. Caminada

2., mit neuen Projekten erweiterte Auflage des Bandes «Cul zuffel e l'aura dado»
2nd edition of *Cul zuffel e l'aura dado*, extended to include new projects

Von Gion A. Caminada ist in der Bündnerischen Surselva ein architektonisches Werk entstanden, das wie kein anderes unmittelbar in den ökonomischen, geografischen und bautechnischen Prämissen eines Ortes und den Lebensgewohnheiten seiner Bevölkerung bedingt ist.
Die neue Buchausgabe umfasst die Texte und die Projektsammlung des Bandes «Cul zuffel e l'aura dado» und ist erweitert um eine Auswahl der neueren Projekte seit 2005.

Gion A. Caminada has produced architectural work in Surselva, Grisons that is unique in being directly determined by the ecological, geographical and structural engineering premises of the location and the lifestyles of its population.
The new edition includes the texts and project collection of *Cul zuffel e l'aura dado* and is extended to include a selection of more recent projects since 2005.

Herausgegeben von / Edited by: Bettina Schlorhaufer
Fotos / Photos: Lucia Degonda
Textbeiträge / Articles by: Gion A. Caminada, Jürg Conzett, Bettina Schlorhaufer, Peter Schmid, Martin Tschanz, Peter Rieder, Walter Zschokke

Ca. / approx. 300 Seiten / pages, 22,5 × 29 cm,
De/En ISBN 978-3-03761-114-2
CHF 138.– / EUR 126.–
Erscheint / Publication: Sommer / Summer 2018

Zürcher Wohnungsbau / Zurich Housing Development 1995–2015

Seit Mitte der 1990er Jahre lässt sich im Grossraum Zürich eine ausserordentliche Qualität von Wohnbauten beobachten. Durch die Förderung der öffentlichen Hand, durch eine hochstehende Wettbewerbskultur und eine rege Architekturszene ist hier ein reichhaltiges Experimentierfeld guter Wohnbauarchitektur entstanden. Das umfangreiche Werk über den Zürcher Wohnungsbau ist eine Anthologie von über 100 Einzelbauten, Ensembles und Siedlungen, die innerhalb von 20 Jahren in der Stadt Zürich entstanden sind. Es ist eine eindrückliche Übersicht zur Wohnbaukultur, die mit ihrer aussergewöhnlichen Qualität eine Intensität und Blüte erlebt, die auch international Beachtung findet.

Housing of exceptional quality has been developed in the greater Zurich area since the mid-1990s. Public funding, the high standard of the competition culture and a vibrant architectural scene have resulted in a rich field of experimentation for good residential architecture. The approximately 500-page volume on Zurich housing construction is an anthology of over 100 individual buildings, ensembles and settlements developed over a period of 20 years. It is an impressive representation of an intense, blossoming housing development culture that has also attracted international attention.

Herausgeber / Edited by: Heinz Wirz, Christoph Wieser

476 Seiten / pages, 24 × 29 cm
710 Abbildungen / illustrations, 713 Pläne / plans
Hardcover, fadengeheftet / thread-stitched
De/En ISBN 978-3-03761-127-2
CHF 138.– / EUR 126.–

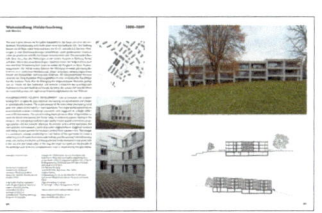

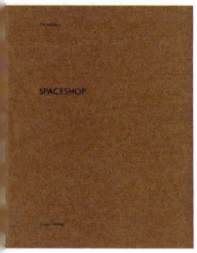 

spaceshop Architekten De aedibus 73

Vier Architekten – Beno Aeschlimann, Stefan Hess, Reto Mosimann und seit 2012 Hanspeter Stauffer – zeichnen verantwortlich für das Büro spaceshop Architekten in Biel. Seit 1998 ist eine beachtliche Reihe von hochspannenden Bauten und Sanierungen entstanden. Darunter etwa die Erweiterung der Volksschule Sonnenhof in Bern, die das Repertoire der «Solothurner Schule» neu und sensibel interpretiert.

Four architects – Beno Aeschlimann, Stefan Hess, Reto Mosimann and, since 2012, Hanspeter Stauffer – are responsible for the Biel office spaceshop Architekten. Since 1998, it has produced an impressive series of highly exciting buildings and renovation projects. They include the extension to the Sonnenhof Primary School in Bern, which reinterprets the repertoire of the "Solothurn school" in a new and sensitive way.

Textbeitrag/Article by: Christoph Schläppi, Bern
92 Seiten/page, 22,5 × 29 cm
Fadengeheftete Broschur/stitched brochure
De/En ISBN 978-3-03761-145-6, CHF 48.–/EUR 44.–

HDPF Anthologie 38

Nikolaus Hamburger, Dario Pfammatter und Francisco Ferrandiz sind die Protagonisten des Zürcher Büros HDPF. Innerhalb weniger Jahre haben die Architekten ein beachtliches Werk geschaffen. Es sind vorrangig Mehrfamilien- und Einfamilienhäuser, die durch ihre konstruktive Klarheit, eine stringente Materialwahl, Plastizität der äusseren Form und ausgeprägte Tektonik bestechen.

Nikolaus Hamburger, Dario Pfammatter and Francisco Ferrandiz are the protagonists of the Zurich office HDPF. Within only a few years, the architects have produced an impressive oeuvre. The projects are mostly apartment buildings and single-family homes that are incisive in terms of their structural clarity, stringent material selection, the sculptural quality of their exterior and their pronounced tectonics.

52 Seiten/pages, 16,5 × 21 cm
Fadengeheftete Broschur/stitched brochure
De/En ISBN 978-3-03761-136-4
CHF 28.–/EUR 25.–

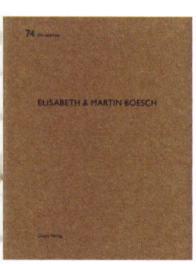 

Elisabeth & Martin Boesch De aedibus 74

Renovation, Umbau, Restaurierung sind anspruchsvolle architektonische Aufgaben, die selten diskutiert werden. Das Zürcher Architektenpaar verfolgt seit Jahren mit grosser Umsicht dieses Thema. So sind einige bemerkenswerte Umbauten und Restaurierungen entstanden. So etwa in Zürich der Umbau Werkhof, die Erweiterung Villa Rainhof, der Umbau Geschäftshaus Homburger oder die Restaurierung der Tonhalle.

Renovation, conversion and restoration are challenging architectural tasks that are seldom discussed. For many years now, the architect couple from Zurich has pursued this topic with great care, creating notable conversions and restorations such as the Zurich projects to convert a maintenance depot, extend the Villa Rainhof, convert the Homburger commercial building and renovate the Tonhalle.

Textbeitrag/Article by: Elisabeth & Martin Boesch, Zürich
96 Seiten/pages, 22,5 × 29 cm
Fadengeheftete Broschur/stitched brochure
De/En ISBN 978-3-03761-006-0, CHF 48.–/EUR 44.–

Beer Merz Anthologie 39

Anja Beer und David Merz gründeten ihr Büro 2010 in Basel. Ihre kleineren Bauten, ein Wohnheim und Sanierungen von Wohnbauten, folgen dem vornehmen Gebot der Rücksicht, des Respekts und der Integration. Ihre intelligent entwickelten Lösungen orientieren sich an der Funktion der Bauten ebenso wie am baulichen Bestand.

Anja Beer and David Merz founded their own office in Basel in 2010. Their smaller buildings, a residential home and housing renovation projects pursue the noble aim of consideration, respect and integration. Their intelligently developed solutions are orientated towards the functions of their buildings and the given existing structures.

60 Seiten/pages, 16,5 × 21 cm
Fadengeheftete Broschur/stitched brochur
De/En ISBN 978-3-03761-160-9
CHF 28.–/EUR 25.–

Analoge Altneue Architektur – Miroslav Šik

Analoge Architektur und Altneue Architektur prägen die Lehre von Miroslav Šik an der ETH Zürich. Seine Architektur, Theorie und Lehre stellen einen spezifischen und relevanten Pfeiler der schweizerischen und europäischen Architektur dar. Der umfangreiche Band enthält insgesamt 135 ausgewählte studentische Projekte aus beiden Phasen, deren etliche Verfasser heute zu den namhaften Schweizer Architekten zählen. Grossformatige perspektivische Zeichnungen, Collagen, Pläne mit Detailtreue und prägnant formulierte Projektbeschreibungen veranschaulichen bildhaft die Methode und deren Ergebnisse. Weiter enthält der Band ein Vorwort von Miroslav Šik, einen ausführlichen Text zu Entstehung und Entwurfsmethode von Lukas Imhof, sowie erhellende Essays und Interviewzitate ehemaliger Schüler zur Analogen und Altneuen Architektur. Eine Sammlung der mit charakteristischem Biss formulierten Entwurfsprogramme und eine bebilderte Darstellung der berühmten und mit Anekdoten behafteten Jaxon-Maltechnik runden diese umfangreiche Projektschau ab.

The terms "analogous architecture" and "old-new architecture" are key aspects of the teaching of Miroslav Šik at the ETH Zurich. Since the 1990s, Šik's theory and teaching have formed an important pillar of Swiss and international architectural history.
This extensive volume contains the best 90/120 works respectively by students from both periods of Miroslav Šik's teaching, including plans, project descriptions and perspective diagrams. Some of the presented students went on to become renowned contemporary Swiss architects. This volume also includes the most important manifesto-like texts by Miroslav Šik and enlightening essays on the movement of analogous and old-new architecture.

Herausgeber / Edited by: Miroslav Šik, Eva Willenegger
Textbeiträge /Articles by: Miroslav Šik, Lukas Imhof, Alberto Dell'Antonio, Andreas Hagmann, Christoph Mathys

472 Seiten / pages, 21 × 29 cm
694 Abbildungen / illustrations, 522 Skizzen und Pläne / sketches and plans
Hardcover, fadengeheftet / thread-stitched
De ISBN 978-3-03761-153-1
En ISBN 978-3-03761-154-8
CHF 128.–/ EUR 116.–

Defining Criteria

Die zwei Herausgeber, Absolventen der Architekturakademie Mendrisio (Università della Svizzera italiana), haben sechs namhafte Architekten und vier bekannte Kunstschaffende der jüngsten Generation nach ihren grundlegenden Motivationen, Ausrichtungen und Haltungen in der Architektur und Kunst befragt. Entstanden sind inspirierende und tief greifende Reflexionen, die begleitet sind von Zitaten, symbolhaften Bildern und Darstellungen von reellen Projekten aus der Welt der Architektur und Kunst, die ihre Ideen und Reflexionen unterstreichen und versinnbildlichen.
Interviewt wurden die Architekten Kersten Geers (Office KGDVS, Brüssel), François Charbonnet (Made in, Genf), Go Hasegawa (Tokio), Anne Holtrop (Bachrain und Amsterdam), Pier Vittorio Aureli und Martino Tattara (DOGMA, Brüssel und London) und Junya Ishigami (Tokio); sowie die Künstler Ila Bêka und Louise Lemoine (Filmemacher, Paris), Philipp Schaerer (Zürich und Steffisburg), Yuri Ancarani (Visueller Künstler und Filmemacher, Mailand) und Bas Princen (Fotograf, Zürich und Rotterdam).

The two editors, graduate architects from the Mendrisio Academy of Architecture (Università della Svizzera italiana) asked six renowned architects and four well-known artists, all among the latest generation in their field, about their underlying motivation, orientation and stances with respect to architecture and art. The result is inspiring, in-depth reflection, enhanced by quotes, symbolic images and presentations of real projects from the world of architecture and art that underline and symbolize their ideas and reflections.
Interviews with the architects Kersten Geers (Office KGDVS, Brussels), François Charbonnet (Made in, Geneva), Go Hasegawa (Tokyo), Anne Holtrop (Bahrain and Amsterdam), Pier Vittorio Aureli and Martino Tattara (DOGMA, Brussels and London), Junya Ishigami (Tokyo) and the artists Ila Bêka and Louise Lemoine (film-makers, Paris), Philipp Schaerer (Zurich and Steffisburg), Yuri Ancarani (visual artist and film-maker, Milan), Bas Princen (photographer, Zurich and Rotterdam).

Herausgeber / Edited by: Stephan Lando, Marina Montresor

296 Seiten / pages, 20 × 27 cm
164 Abbildungen / illustrations
Fadengeheftete Freirückenbroschur / Thread-stitched lay-flat brochure
De ISBN 978-3-03761-172-2
En ISBN 978-3-03761-173-9
CHF 54.–/ EUR 49.–

Walter Angonese – Kaltern/Caldaro De aedibus international 14

Mit jeder Bauaufgabe betreibt der Südtiroler Architekt eine grundsätzliche architektonische Recherche und gelangt damit zu präzisen, eigenständigen Lösungen. Abstraktion, Konstruktion, Poesie sind dabei Konstanten in seinem Werk.

The buildings by the South Tyrolean architect are all works with a sophisticated structure and a close relationship to the existing buildings and the location, with its various parameters. The building, topography, perimeter walls and neighbouring structures are closely interwoven, thereby creating new, powerful overall images.

Textbeitrag/Article by: Arno Ritter, Innsbruck
72 Seiten/pages, 22,5 × 29 cm
Fadengeheftete Broschur/stitched brochure
De/En ISBN 978-3-03761-121-0, CHF 48.–/EUR 44.–

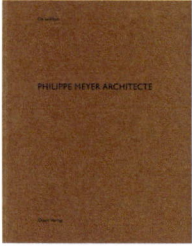 

Philippe Meyer De aedibus 71

Transparenz und solide Konstruktion ergänzen und bedingen sich in Philippe Meyers Projekten gegenseitig. Der Band bildet einen Querschnitt durch seine markanten Projekte ab, die seit 2003 entstanden sind, so unter anderem ausladende Villen rund um Genf, das neue Physikgebäude der Universität Genf oder etwa ein Wohngebäude für Studenten in Montreux.

Transparency and solid construction complement and depend on each other in the projects by Philippe Meyer. The volume presents a cross-section of the precisely defined projects that have been executed since 2003. They include expansive villas in the regional round Geneva, the new Physics Building of the University of Geneva or a residential building for students in Montreux.

Textbeiträge/Articles by: Paolo Amaldi, Genf; Philippe Meyer, Genf; Jacques Sbriglio, Aix-en-Provence
104 Seiten/pages, 22,5 × 29 cm
Fadengeheftete Broschur/stitched brochure
De/En/Fr ISBN 978-3-03761-152-4, CHF 48.–/EUR 44.–

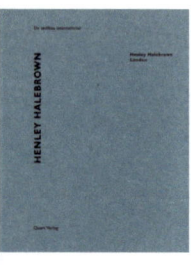 

Henley Halebrown – London De aedibus international 15

Die herrschenden sozialen Strukturen und die kulturellen und architektonischen Eigenheiten des Ortes sind für Simon Henley und Gavin Hale-Brown Inspiration für ihre Entwürfe. Der Band stellt einige Bauten vor, die nicht selten ins dichte Stadtgewebe Londons eingespannt sind und eine ebenso selbstbehauptende wie poetische Ausstrahlung haben.

Designs by Simon Henley and Gavin Hale-Brown are inspired by the dominant social structures of the location as well as its cultural and architectural characteristics. This volume presents a number of buildings that are often inserted into the dense urban texture of London with a self-assertive, poetic expression.

Textbeitrag/Article by: Hugh Strange, London
64 Seiten/pages, 22,5 × 29 cm
Fadengeheftete Broschur/stitched brochure
De/En ISBN 978-3-03761-159-3, CHF 48.–/EUR 44.–

Kast Kaeppeli De aedibus 72

Die beiden Berner Architekten Adrian Kast und Thomas Kaeppeli gründeten ihr Büro – mit einer Zweigstelle in Basel – 2008. Ihre Bauten sind im Grundriss, im Schnitt und in der Konstruktion wohl durchdachte, raffiniert entwickelte Preziosen. Beispielhaft stehen hierfür verschiedene Wohnhäuser, drei Kindergärten und mehrere Schulhäuser.

The two Bern-based architects Adrian Kast and Thomas Kaeppeli founded offices in 2008, including a branch in Basel. In terms of their floor plan, section and construction, their buildings are well-considered, precise structures that have been developed in a sophisticated way: for instance, various residential buildings, three kindergartens and several school buildings.

Textbeiträge/Articles by: Tibor Joanelly, Zürich; Christoph Schläppi, Bern
80 Seiten/pages, 22,5 × 29 cm
Fadengeheftete Broschur/stitched brochure
De/En ISBN 978-3-03761-157-9, CHF 48.–/EUR 44.–

Betonfertigteilen – Stützen und Balken – gefügt. Sein Aufbau schafft, bei aller Differenz, strukturell wie im Ausdruck, Nähe zum Hauptbau. Beide sind ähnlich «weich». Derselbe Anbau in Ortbeton wäre markant weniger planungsintensiv gewesen und seine Herstellung weniger aufwendig und schneller realisierbar, aber auch zu sehr auf sich selbst bezogen, zu hart.

Innere Räume
Sie sind fragil, sie werden als Erstes verändert, oft schon nach kürzester Zeit. Und doch sind sie es, die verantwortlich sind für eine bestimmte Stimmung, eine jeweilige Atmosphäre. Entwickelt, untersucht, überprüft werden sie mit Perspektiven oder in Modellen im Massstab 1:33. Licht und Schatten sind das eine, mehr interessiert uns das reiche Zusammenspiel von Licht, Materialität und Farbigkeit. Letztere ist immer dabei, sei sie nun unmittelbar wahr- und benennbar oder nur still vorhanden, ganz nebenbei. Die Farbigkeit ist jedesmal neu zu erarbeiten und neu zu bestimmen. Sie verdeutlicht die Struktur des Grundrisses (Praxis Dr. Z in Schwamendingen), veredelt und verfremdet Materialien (Praxis Dr. A. in Zürich), suggeriert ein Festzelt (Kurtheater Baden), überspielt Störungen und dramatisiert räumliche Tiefenwirkung (Schuhläden Arode), erzeugt heftig leuchtend heitere Festlichkeit (Expo-Pavillon), dient hingehaucht zur Individualisierung von Räumen (Villa Rainhof), ist wegleitend und orientiert (Bürogebäude, Eggbühl), demonstriert die atmosphärische Wandelbarkeit bestehender innerer Räume (EPI-Klinik, Zürich), verbindet Alt und Neu (Villa Rainhof), betont historische und räumliche Kontinuität und höht Materialität (UNO, New York), taugt als Gegenkonzept zu edler Materialisierung und forcierter Detaillierung (Bürogebäude, Eggbühl), veredelt diskret mittels Schablonenmalerei mit farblosem Glanzlack (Expo-Pavillon, Ausstellung im Architektur Forum Zürich, Villa Rainhof), wird entdeckt und wiederhergestellt (Atelierhaus Kind, Riehen), zitiert *friendly competitors* (Expo-Pavillon) oder schärft die Wahrnehmung des Raumes entgegen der erklärten Absicht des Architekten (im Deutschen Architekturmuseum, Frankfurt am Main für die Dauer der Ausstellung «Schweizerische Architektur im 20. Jahrhundert») oder ist materialbedingt (Läden für Jil Sander u. a.).

Produktiver Ungehorsam
Verschiedene Umbauprojekte sind Resultate eines produktiven Ungehorsams – nicht als Ziel, sondern aus Notwendigkeit. Das Risiko, das man dabei in Wettbewerben in Kauf nimmt, hat sich mit den neuen Rekursmöglichkeiten, einer neuen Rekurslust, im

responsible for a specific mood, a respective atmosphere. They are developed, studied and tested using perspectives or 1:33 scale models. Light and shadow are one aspect, but the rich interplay of light, materials and colours is at least as interesting. Colours are always a factor, either clearly perceived and defined, or silently present, almost casually. Colour concepts have to be newly developed and defined every time. They clarify the structure of the floor plan (Dr. Z's practice in Schwamendingen), refine and alienate materials (Dr. A's practice in Zurich), hint at a festive tent (Stadtsaal Baden), cover distractions and dramatise the spatial effect of depth (shoes shops, Arode), create radiant, joyful festivity (Expo pavilion), subtly serve to individualise rooms (Villa Rainhof), provide guidance and orientation (Eggbühl commercial building), demonstrate the atmospheric convertibility of existing interior spaces (EPI Zurich), connect old and new elements (Villa Rainhof), highlight historical and spatial continuity and enhance materials (UN NY), can be used as a counter-concept to refined materiality and forced detail (Eggbühl commercial building), discreetly add refinement using stencil painting with colourless, glossy varnish (Expo pavilion, exhibition in the Architektur Forum Zurich, Villa Rainhof), are discovered and restored (Kind studio home), quote *friendly competitors* (Expo pavilion), heighten the perception of space in contradiction to the architect's declared intentions (Deutsche Architekturmuseum, Frankfurt for the period of the exhibition *Schweizerische Architektur im 20. Jahrhundert*), or depend on the materials used (Jil Sander and others).

Productive disobedience
Some of our conversion projects have been the result of productive disobedience – not as an aim, but out of necessity. The risk this entails in competitions has drastically increased with public procurement regulations, new recourse possibilities and an increasing readiness to recourse – possibly at the expense of a better solution. In the case of the youth hostel by Ernst Gisel in Zurich, the local problem of a small replacement building led to the entire overhaul of an already existing project by third parties. The interface problems evoked by the prize-winning design proved to be unsolvable and led us to drop the project. Another project for the EPI Zurich was intended to include preserving an existing building, which dated back to its foundation, and the cafeteria by Bruno Giacometti rather than demolishing them and replacing them with a new restaurant. Debate was heated and the reassessment led to a new solution by other architects. A further example is the

Vergabewesen der öffentlichen Hand drastisch erhöht – möglicherweise zuungunsten der besseren Lösung. Im Fall der Jugendherberge in Zürich von Ernst Gisel wurde aus dem lokalen Problem eines kleinen Ersatzbaus die Gesamtüberarbeitung eines Projektes von Dritten. Das mit dem preisgekrönten Entwurf evozierte Schnittstellenproblem erwies sich als unlösbar und liess uns das Projekt abgeben. Das Projekt für die EPI-Klinik in Zürich sah anstelle des Abbruchs eines Gründerhauses und der Cafeteria von Bruno Giacometti sowie des Neubaus eines Restaurants den Erhalt und Umbau des Bestandes vor. Die Diskussionen waren heftig und das Umdenken führte zu einer neuen Lösung durch Dritte. Nicht Leichtfertigkeit, sondern Erfahrung und tiefes Verständnis für das Besondere an Lisbeth Sachs' Kurtheater in Baden führten zwingend zur überzeugenden, jedoch riskanten, weil gegen die denkmalpflegerische Vorgabe verstossenden Integration des Sachsfoyers in das neue Foyer. Anstelle der geforderten zwei vereinzelten Foyers entfaltet sich das Alte zu einem einzigen neuen Ganzen.

Eine geborgte Weisheit, gültig für alle Massstäbe
«Wer von einem wertvollen alten Baum frische Früchte will, wird nicht den Gärtner schätzen, der vorschlägt, ihn umzuhauen und einen neuen zu pflanzen, sondern den, der den alten Stamm so behandelt, dass er neue fruchtbare Zweige treibt.
Und deshalb kann man das Problem der Grossstadt nicht anfassen aus allgemeiner Theorie heraus, sondern nur durch das liebevolle Versenken in das Wesen einer bestimmten Stadt, der praktische Arbeit gelten soll. Je eigenartiger diese bestimmte Stadt ist, um so mehr wird man den Schlüssel zu ihrer Behandlung in dieser Eigenart suchen müssen.»[8]

Elisabeth und Martin Boesch im August 2009

[8] Fritz Schumacher in *Das Werden einer Wohnstadt*. Hamburgische Hausbibliothek, Hamburg: Georg Westermann 1932. S. 12

extension of the stately villa in Rämistrasse 66, Zurich, to accommodate a library (see above). In Appenzell, the requirement to preserve a building that is no longer used and can in urban planning terms be regarded as merely an interim solution dating back to the period of through-traffic, provoked contradiction. The revised church base, instead of a pedestrian gallery, clarifies the profile of the street space and convinced the competition jury. Not levity, but experience and a deep understanding for the special nature of Lisbeth Sachs' Kurtheater in Baden inevitably led to the convincing, yet risky measure (since it contravened monumental preservation requirements) of integrating the Sachsfoyer into the new foyer. Instead of the requested two individual foyers, the old unfolds into a single, new unit.

A borrowed piece of wisdom that applies to all scales
"Those who seek fresh fruit from a valuable old tree will not care for the gardener who suggests chopping it down and planting a new one. Instead, he appreciates one that advises treating the old trunk in a way that induces new branches to sprout. And that is why one cannot grasp the problem of major cities from a position of pure theory, but must lovingly immerse oneself into the nature of a specific city to which practical work will be applied. The more unique the specific city is, the more one must seek the key to its treatment in that very uniqueness."[8]

Elisabeth and Martin Boesch, August 2009

[8] Fritz Schumacher in *Das Werden einer Wohnstadt*. Hamburgische Hausbibliothek, Hamburg: Georg Westermann 1932. p. 12 [trans.]

März 2018: Die Fünf Regeln des Weiterbauens

1. Die Identität des bestehenden Gebäudes ist zu stärken.
2. Für jede Frage ist die Antwort zuerst im Katalog der Elemente und Regeln zu suchen, welche die Architektur des bestehenden Gebäudes bestimmen.
3. Ergibt Punkt 2 keine Antwort, so ist sie aus der inneren Logik der Architektur des bestehenden Gebäudes zu entwickeln.
4. Jede Frage ist nach diesen Spielregeln abzuwickeln. Ausnahmen erfordern Argumente. Gestalterische Automatismen und Klischees sind zu unterlassen.
5. Der Zweifel sei treuer Begleiter.

Die Synthese
Weiterbauen: Das Bestehende weiterentwickeln nach dessen eigenen Regeln – durch umsichtiges Interpretieren derselben.

March 2018: Five rules for the architectural work on existing buildings (continued buidling)

1. Reinforce the identity of the existing building.
2. The answer to every question should be sought in the catalogue of elements and rules established by the architecture of the existing building.
3. If rule number 2 does not give an answer, it should be developed out of the internal logic of the existing building.
4. For every question, the answer should be sought following the same rules of play. Exceptions need arguments. Omit every automatism and cliché.
5. Doubt should be your continuous companion.

Synthesis
Continued building: continue with the rules of the existing structures, interpreting them cautiously.

1999 Wettbewerb Stadtsaal, Baden
1999 Competition, Stadtsaal, Baden

2002 Studienauftrag Restaurant EPL Klinik, Zürich
2002 Study contract, EPL Clinic restaurant, Zurich

2007 Studienauftrag Erweiterung Kurtheater, Baden
2007 Study contract, Kurtheater extension, Baden

2007 Studie Erweiterung ZHAW, Winterthur
2007 Study, ZHAW extension, Winterthur

2002–2003 Geschenk der Schweiz an die UNO, New York
2002–2003 Swiss gift to the UN, New York

1990 Studie für Jil Sander, Hamburg
1990 Study for Jil Sander, Hamburg

Um- und Anbau Haus B-T, Feldmeilen

Conversion and extension of B-T house, Feldmeilen

Baujahr / Year of construction: 1947
Direktauftrag / Direct commission: 1982
Ausführung / Construction measure: 1983–1984
Bauingenieur / Civil engineer: Santiago Calatrava Valls, Zürich
Auftraggeber / Client: privat / private

Nach der Verkleinerung der Familie wird das Haus aufgeteilt und eine Einliegerwohnung gewonnen. Dazu werden zwei Türöffnungen zugemauert und ein schmales und ein breites Fenster zu Durchgängen in den Anbau geöffnet. Er enthält die Infrastruktur, bestehend aus Eingang mit Garderobeschrank, Küche, Dusche/WC. Zwischen Haus und Grenzabstand steht für den Anbau ein Landstreifen von 1.5 m Breite zur Verfügung: Es resultiert ein Baukörper von derselben Breite, 10 m Länge, 6 m Höhe, ergänzt mit zwei Erkern. Ein paar Stichworte: Der Beton des Sockels ist grau wie der gestrichene Sockel des Hauses, die schmale Chaletschalung weiss gestrichen wie der Verputz des Hauses; sein einfacher Ausbau wiederum findet sich auch im Anbau; die Fenstergliederung des Küchenerkers dehnt dessen perspektivische Wahrnehmung; seine Ausdrehung beugt die Sicht in die Tiefe des Nachbargartens; das Oberlicht an der Nordwestecke lässt morgens und wiederum abends Sonnenlicht ins Bad; das Lochblech mit runder Auslassung vor dem Dusche/WC-Fenster verweist auf die einfach-dekorativen Fenstergitter am Haus; Differenzierung statt Reduktion. Das Haus und die neue Wohnung haben je einen eigenen Zugang und Gartenbereich. Kleine Architekturen im Garten, sie deuten eine Vielzahl von Möglichkeiten an, widerspiegeln die innere Aufteilung im Äusseren.

After a family reduced in size, the house was divided to create an annexe apartment. To do so, two doors were filled in, while one narrow and one broad window were opened to become passages to the extension. It houses the infrastructure, consisting of an entrance with a cloakroom closet, a kitchen and a shower/WC. A 1.50 m wide strip of land is available for the extension between the existing house and the required distance to the neighbouring properties: the result is a volume with the same breadth, 10 m length, a 6 m height, plus two bay windows. Key facts: the concrete base is grey, like the painted base of the existing house. The narrow timber cladding is painted white, like the plaster of the existing house. Its simple finishing is reflected in the extension. The alignment of the kitchen bay window lengthens its apparent perspective. Its twisted form guides the view into the depth of the neighbouring garden. The skylight on the northwest corner provides light for the small bathroom in the morning and evening. The perforated sheet metal with a round outlet in front of the shower/WC window refers to the common decorative window grilles of the existing house. Distinction rather than reduction. The house and the new apartment each have their own entrance and access to the garden. Small architectural measures in the garden – implying a wide range of possibilities – reflect the inner partition outside.

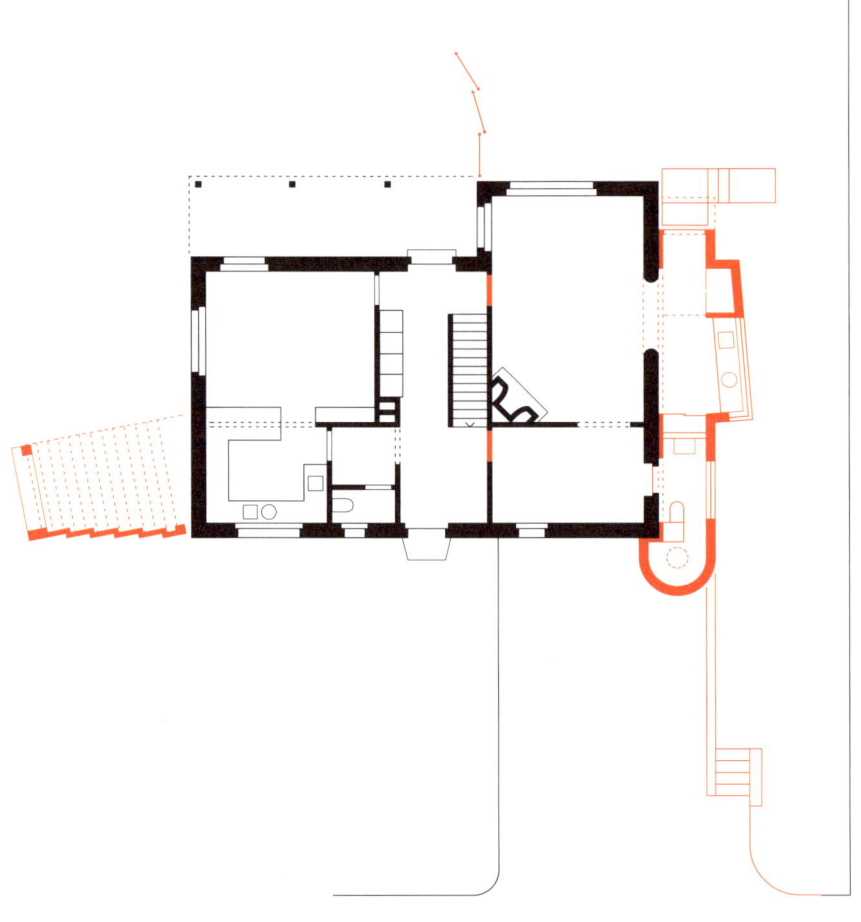

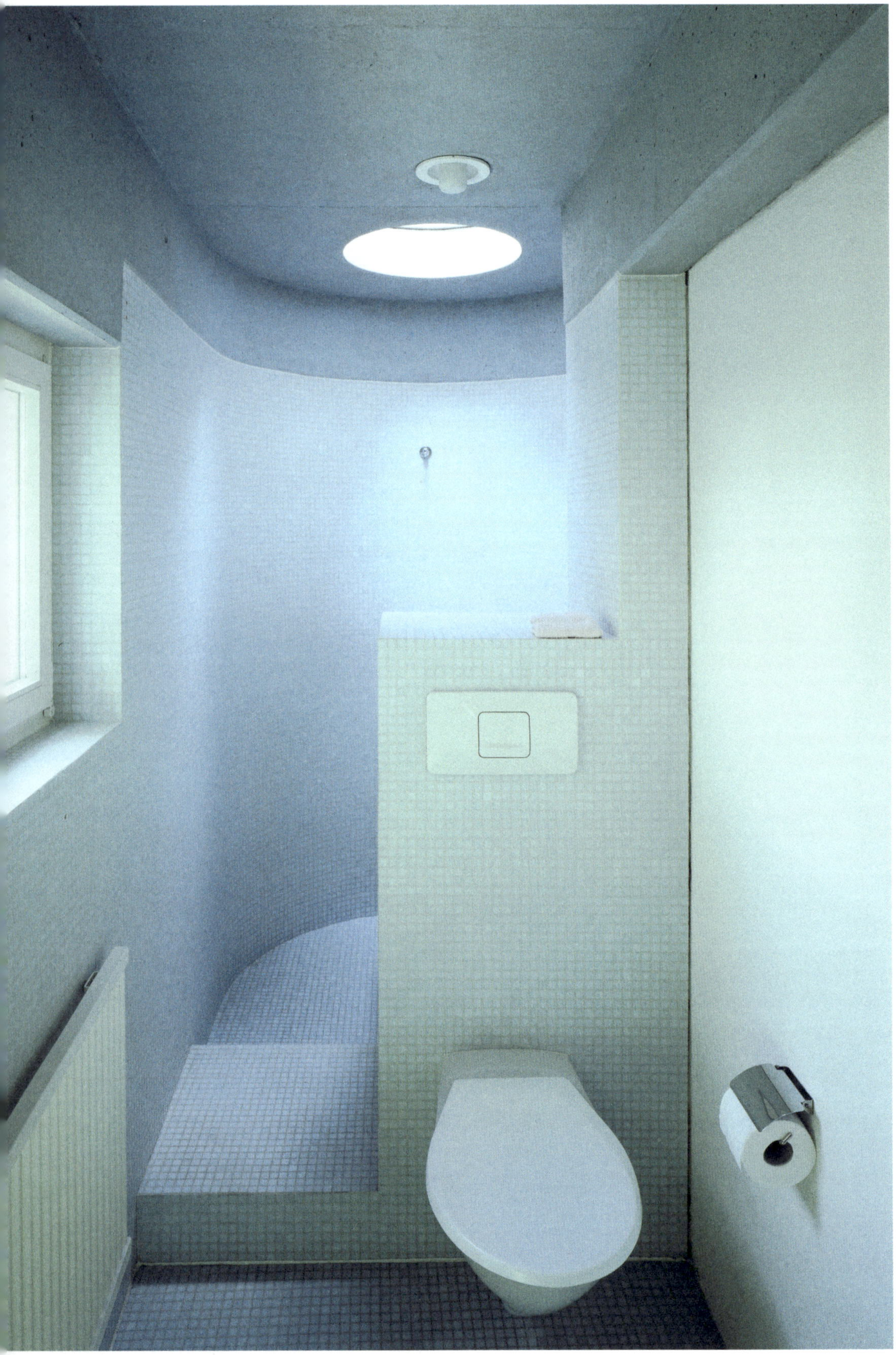

Umbauten in Berlin, Tokio, Hongkong etc.

Conversions in Berlin, Tokyo, Hong Kong etc.

Direktauftrag / Direct commission: 1985
Ausführung / Construction measures:
Hamburg 1985, St. Moritz 1985–1986,
Gstaad 1987, Bern 1987, Genf / Geneva
1986, Stuttgart 1988–1989, Hannover
1987, Düsseldorf 1988, Berlin 1987–1990,
Tokio Aoyama 1989–1991, Tokio New
Otani 1990–1991, Hongkong 1990
Auftraggeber / Client: Jil Sander,
Franchise-Partner

Das räumlich schwer zu bändigende erste Ladenlokal generiert eine eigene Entwurfsstrategie. Dies erweist sich als Vorteil für alle späteren Läden. Bereits für den Prototyp in Hamburg – diesen ersten von zwölf Aufträgen verdanken wir der Grosszügigkeit von Roger Diener – sind nicht nur ein Material- und Farbkonzept mit einem Katalog von standardisierten Elementen zu entwickeln, sondern ebenso ortsspezifische Massnahmen. Es werden wenige edle Materialien eingesetzt, die gut altern (Jil Sanders Idee einer langlebigen Mode kommt unseren Vorstellungen vom Bauen entgegen): Travertin, Baubronze, Stucco lucido, Gips und Ortbeton. Bis auf die Teile aus Baubronze wird alles vor Ort hergestellt.

Standardisierte Elemente sind das Kleiderregal (ein System von auswechselbaren Teilen), Umkleidekabine (Paravent aus plissiertem Lochblech), Vitrine, grosser und kleiner Spiegel (alles aus Baubronze), ein Tisch sowie Türen für Umkleide- und Nebenräume. Die dem jeweiligen Lokal eigenen räumlichen Probleme werden mit den ortsspezifischen Massnahmen geregelt. Sie sind von Fall zu Fall neu zu konzipieren. Dazu wird Ortbeton verwendet, roh, geschliffen, gestockt. Das Raue, Ungenaue des vorwiegend dem Raumgefüge dienenden Betons steht in absichtvoll komplementärer Beziehung zur Schärfe der Bronzearbeiten. Die gewählte Strategie bewährt sich in weiteren elf Läden, wo dieselben betrieblichen, räumlichen und ausführungsmässigen Qualitäten sowie Wiedererkennbarkeit erwartet werden. Diese, so ist zu vermuten, spielt auf der Ebene einer Raumstimmung, einer «Raumtemperatur». Nun gibt es im Rahmen selbst dieser bescheidenen Aufgabe Gegebenheiten, die den Umbau in Hongkong auch chinesisch, die beiden in Tokio auch japanisch machen. Dieses «auch» kann nicht in formaler Annäherung und Anleihe liegen, sondern es ist in räumlichen Beziehungen enthalten: den drei Läden liegt eine für europäische Wahrnehmung jeweils unsichtbare Figur zugrunde.

The original location was difficult to tackle and generated its own design strategy, which however proved to be an advantage for all subsequent stores. Even for the prototype in Hamburg – we are grateful for the generosity of Roger Diener for the first of twelve commissions – the material and colour concept was developed with a catalogue of standardised elements, as well as measures that were specific to the location. A few fine materials are used that age well (Jil Sander's idea of long-life fashion matches our ideas of construction): travertine, construction bronze, stucco lucido, plaster and cast-in-place concrete. Apart from the elements of construction bronze, everything is produced on-site. Standardised elements include the clothes shelving (a system of exchangeable parts), changing cubicles (screens made of pleated, perforated sheets), show cabinets, small and large mirrors (all made of construction bronze), a table, as well as doors for the changing cubicles and auxiliary rooms. The spatial problems relevant to the location are solved using locally specific measures. They must be newly designed from case to case. Raw, polished and granulated cast-in-place concrete is used. The coarse, imprecise nature of the concrete, which mainly serves the spatial structure, has a deliberately complementary relationship with the sharp bronze work. The chosen strategy has been tried and tested in eleven other stores, where the same operational, spatial and implementation qualities are required, as well as the aspect of recognition. It is assumed to be based on the level of the spatial mood or "temperature". Even within the scope of such modest tasks as these, there are elements that make the conversion in Hong Kong also Chinese, the two conversions in Tokyo also Japanese. This "not only but also" aspect cannot be based on a formal approach or borrowing. Instead it is reflected in spatial relationships. To European eyes, the three stores are respectively based on an invisible figure.

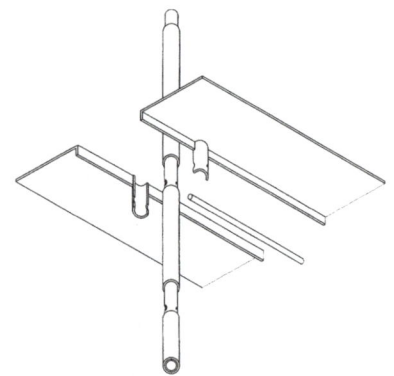

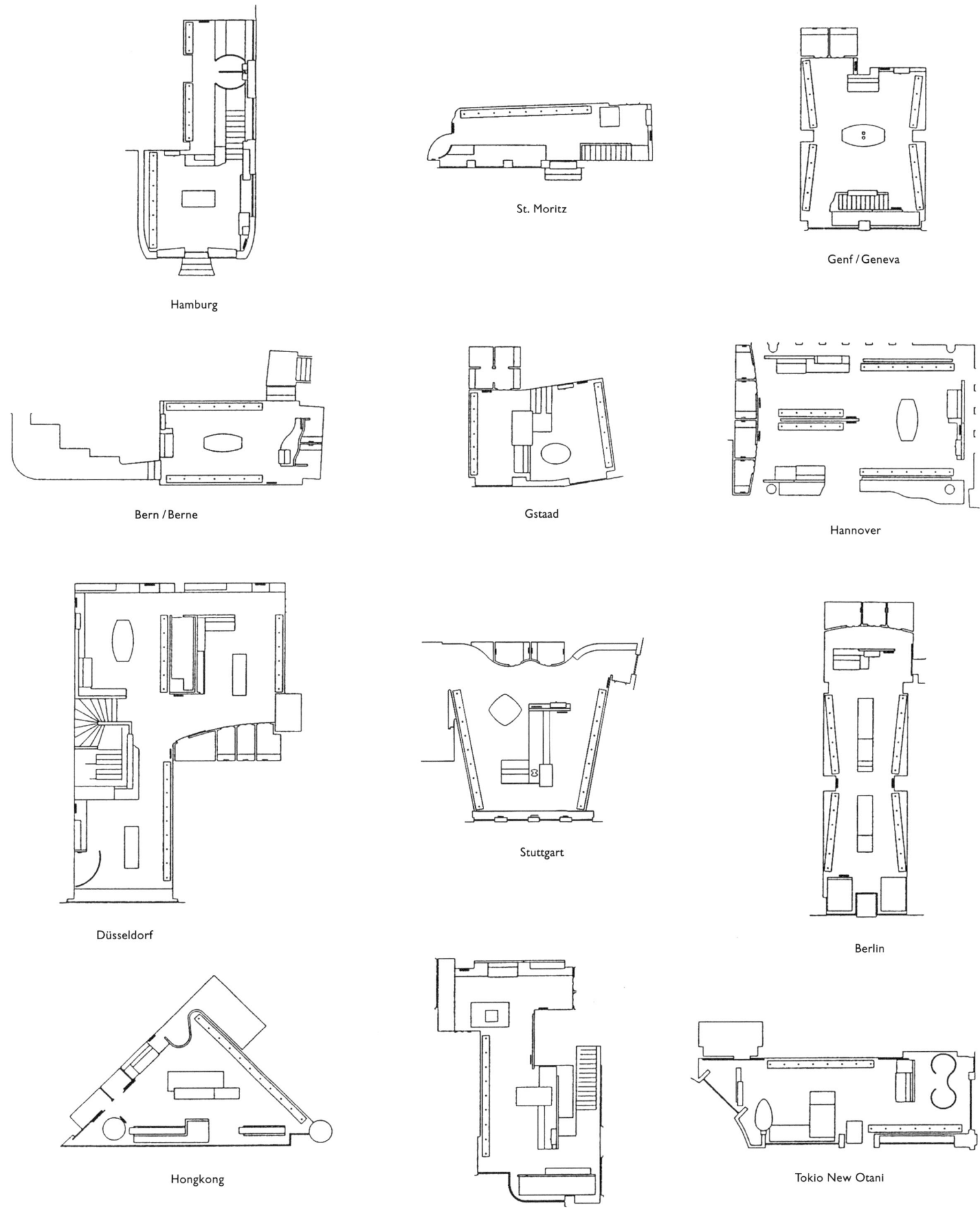

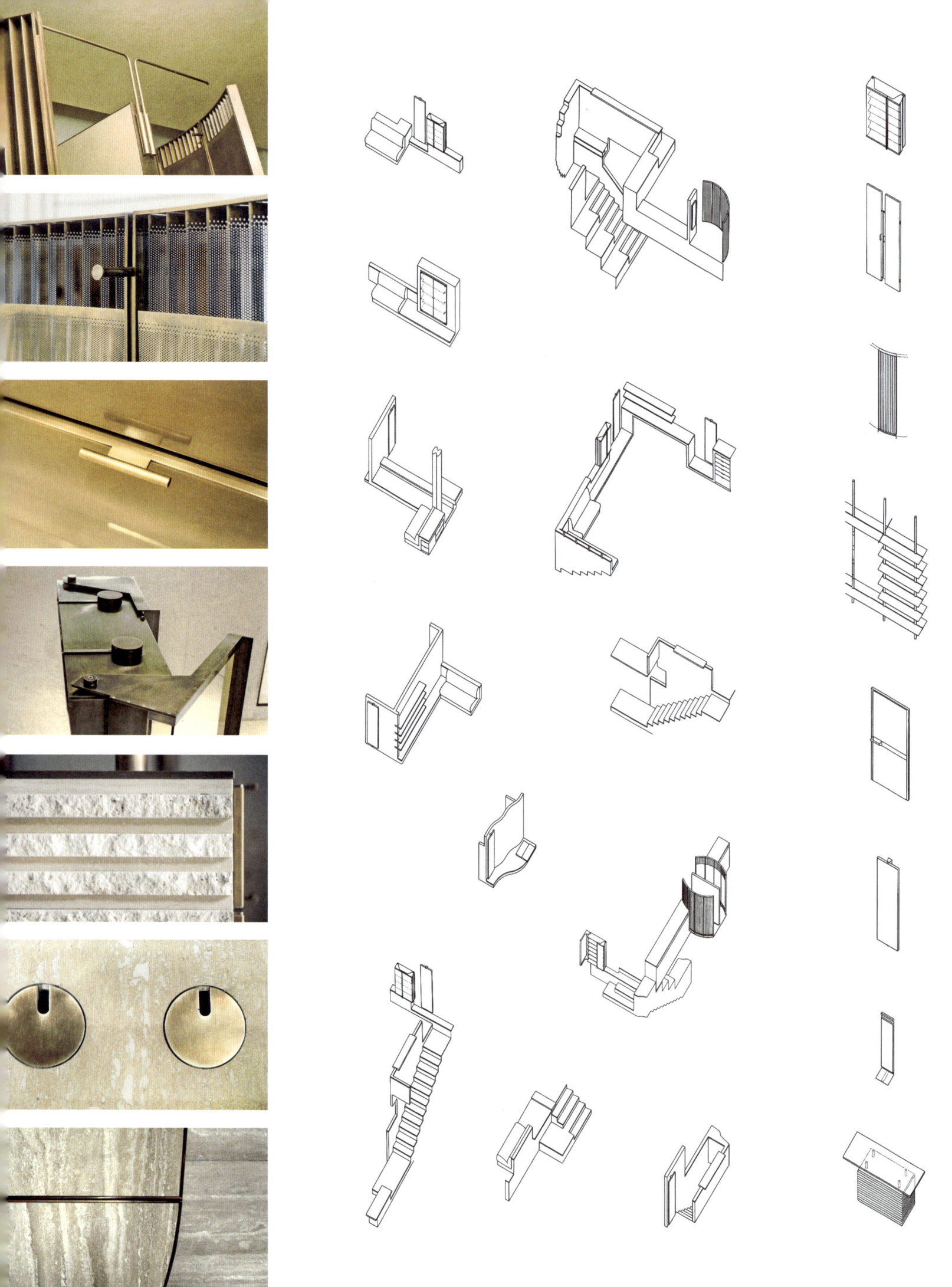

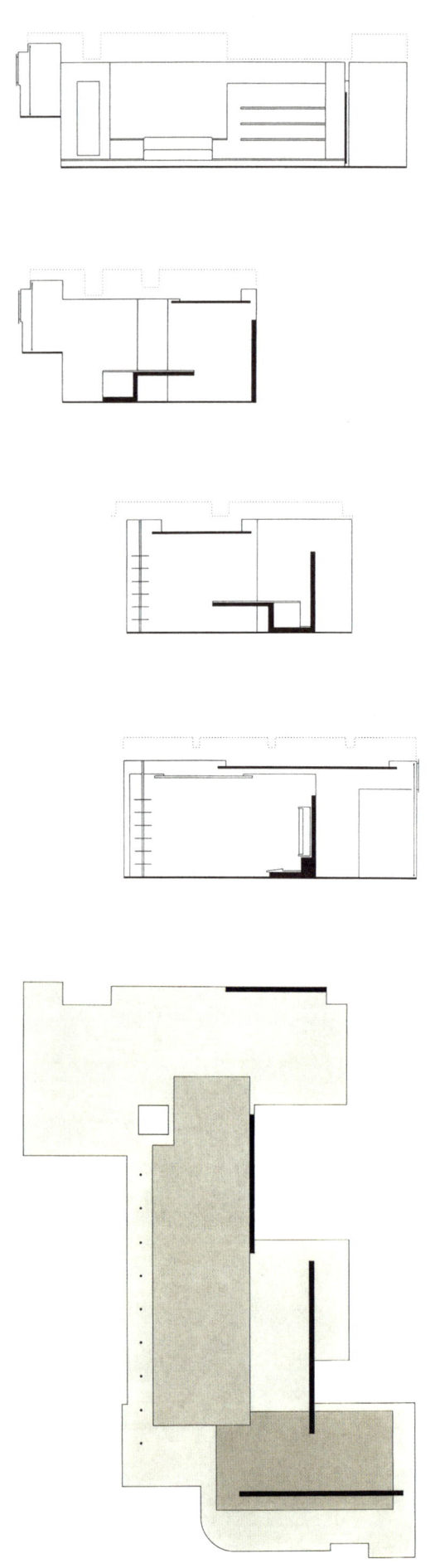

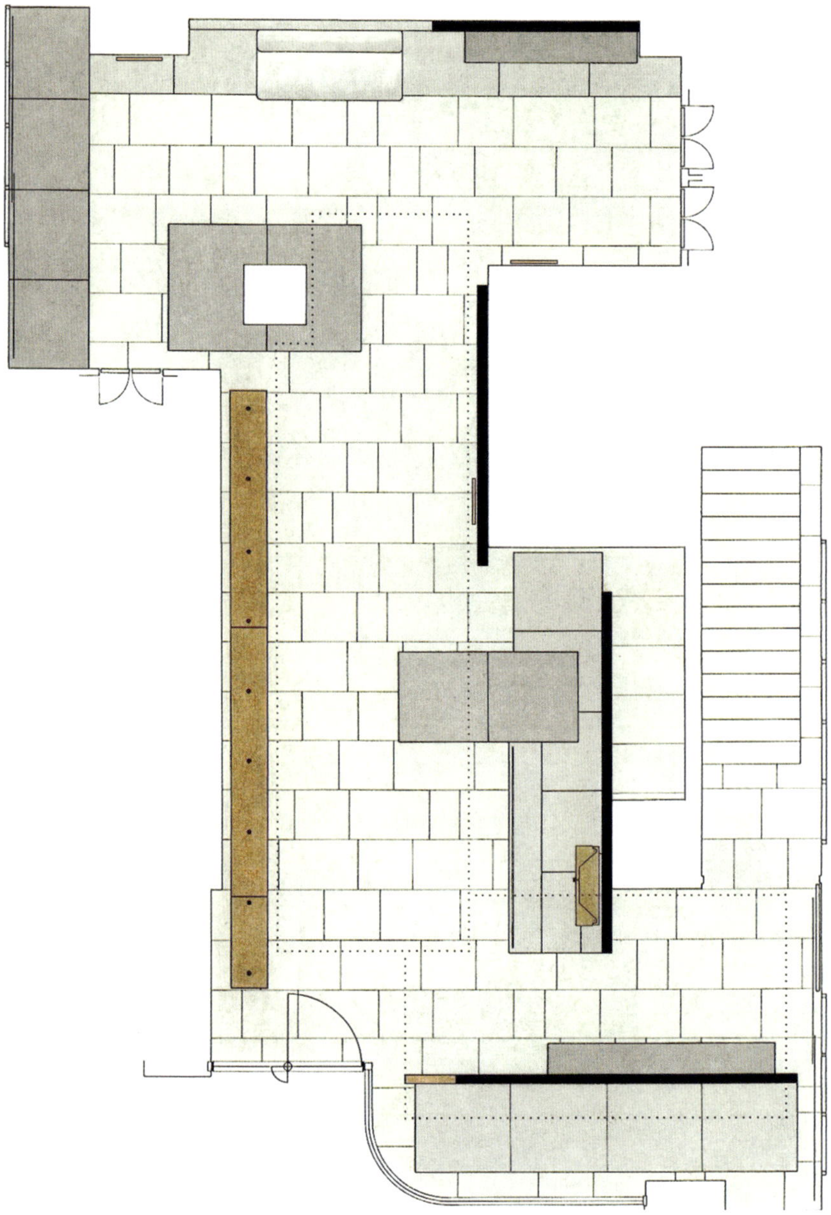

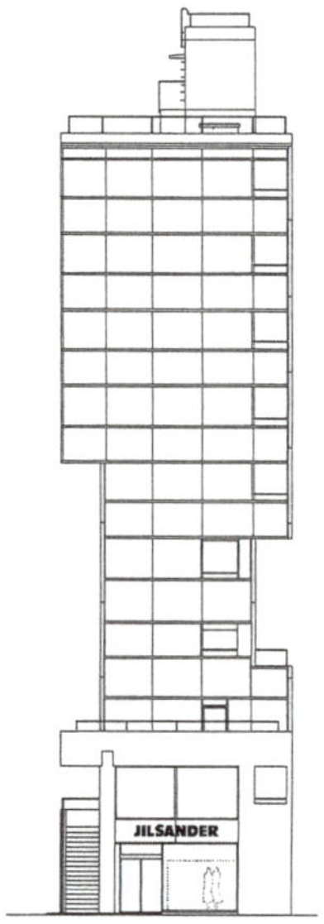

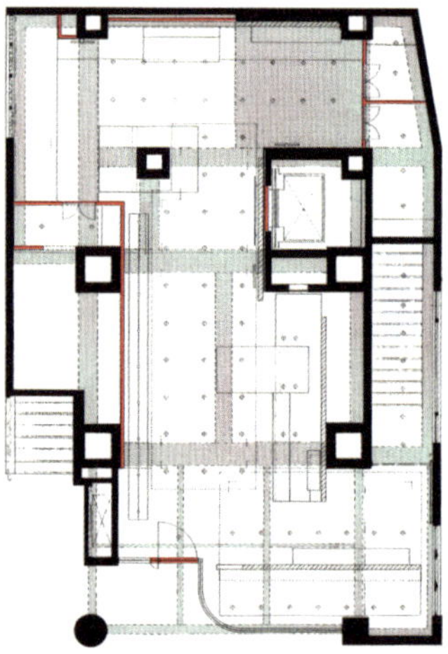

Drei Umbauten, Basel, Lausanne

Three conversions, Basel, Lausanne

Direktauftrag / Direct commission:
September 1989
Ausführung / Construction measure:
Dezember 1989–März 1990 /
December 1989–March 1990
Auftraggeber / Client: privat / private

Für das Erstellen von Schuhläden waren Spielregeln zu erarbeiten. Die Läden sollten schnell zu bauen, billig und wiedererkennbar sein. Erproben liess sich dies an drei Lokalen: eines schmal, tief und niedrig, ein anderes L-förmig und das dritte nahezu quadratisch, hoch, mit einer frei stehenden Stütze. Die Ladenfront war beizubehalten.

Das Prinzip ist denkbar einfach: Wände und Decken des Lokales werden ultramarinblau gestrichen und erzeugen so einen in seiner Weite und Tiefe nicht eindeutig erfassbaren dunklen und konturlosen Raum. In diesen werden helle Platten eingefügt: grossflächige Wand- und Deckenelemente, die sich gegenseitig nicht berühren, mattweissgrau lackiert. Nahezu unabhängig von der nachthimmelähnlichen Raumhülle schaffen sie präzise Raumsituationen, nicht kammerartige, sondern sogenannte fliessende; Raumdichten und Raumproportionen werden durch die Beziehung der horizontalen und vertikalen Platten bestimmt.

Obige Grundregel wird durch gebeizte Sperrholztafeln ergänzt: Dem dunklen fliehenden Blau und dem durch seine Leuchtdichte aktiven Weissgrau wird bei den Durchgängen zum rückwärtigen Lager das körperhafte Rotorange entgegengesetzt. Diese Tafeln agieren als Repoussoir.

Die inszenierte Abfolge von Schaufensterbereich im Vordergrund, einer Wandplatte mit «Vitrine» im Hintergrund und der rotorangenen Sperrholztafel in der Tiefe wird durch das Tag- und insbesondere durch das Nachtlicht dramatisiert.

Hinzu kommen Spiegel, Hocker, «Vitrine» und Schubladenfronten aus massivem Alublech, matt. Auch hier gibt es kein Kultivieren des Details: Die Holz- bzw. Blechplatten sind stumpf gefügt. Die funktionelle Spezifizierung der Wand- und Deckenplatten sowie Bank, Tisch, Spiegel, Hocker und ein Sperrholzteller für das Kleingeld machen das Ganze als Schuhladen brauchbar.

Guidelines had to be developed to build shoe stores. The stores had to be constructed quickly and cheaply, while being recognisable. This could be tested in three locations: one was small, deep and low, one was L-shaped and the third was almost square, high, with a free-standing column. The storefront had to be maintained.

The principle is very simple: the location's walls and ceilings are painted ultramarine to create a dark space without any contours, in which it is difficult to assess the breadth or depth. Bright plates are inserted into it: large scale wall and ceiling elements that do not touch each other and are painted matte light grey. Almost independent of the room's nocturnal sky-like shell, they create precise spatial situations that flow instead of having the character of a chamber. Spatial densities and proportions are defined by the relationship between the horizontal and vertical plates.

The above basic rule is complemented with varnished plywood panels: the dark, fleeing blue and the radiant density of the active grey-white is used as a contrast to the bodily red-orange of the large plywood panels hiding the storage areas at the rear. These panels act as a repoussoir.

The staged sequence of shop window in the foreground, a wall plate with a "showcase" in the background and the red-orange plywood panel in the depths are dramatised by daylight and especially at night.

Mirrors, stools, the "show cabinet" and the drawer fronts are made of solid, matte aluminium sheeting. Here too, no refinement of details: the wood and sheeting plates have butt joints. The functional specification of the wall and ceiling plates, as well as the bench, table, mirror, stool and a plywood disk for small change, make the place convenient as a shoe shop.

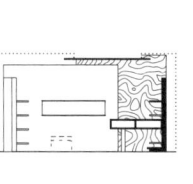
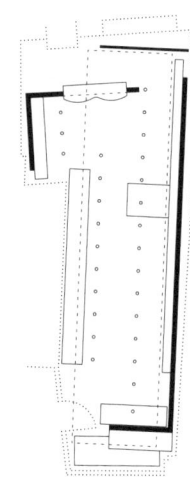
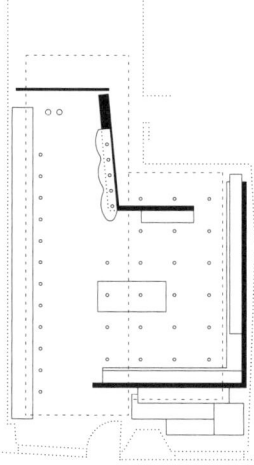
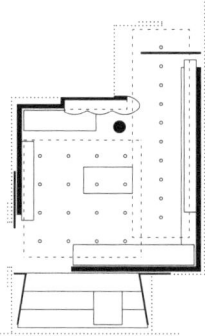

Neuausbau eines Geschäftshauses, Zürich

New interior work for a commercial building, Zurich

Baujahr / Year of construction: 1972
Architekt / Architect: A. Koella, Zürich
Direktauftrag / Direct commission: 1991
Ausführung / Construction measure: 1992–1993
Kunst / Artwork: Sol LeWitt
Auftraggeber / Client: Homburger Rechtsanwälte, Zürich

Zu den wohl noch längere Zeit funktionstüchtigen Elementen der Stadt gehören die Geschäftshäuser der 1960er- und 1970er-Jahre. Die damals unbedingt verlangte Flexibilität der Nutzung und damit die bauliche Trennung von Tragstruktur und Ausbauteilen erweist sich heute als Chance, solche Torsi von innen her zu revitalisieren. Der pragmatische Grundriss, teils dreibündig, teils zur offenen Matrix tendierend, ist offen für mehrere Lesarten. Die angedeutete Windmühlenform erklärt sich weniger aus einer gestalterischen Absicht als aus dem Optimieren der Funktion (Zellenbüros, Gruppenräume) und des Gebäudekörpers innerhalb von Grundstück und Gelände. Der Bau ist klimatisiert, die Geschosshöhen sind minimiert. Der Ausbau vermag den Ansprüchen (technischer, feuerpolizeilicher, organisatorischer und gestalterischer Art) nicht mehr zu genügen. Die Leistungsfähigkeit eines solchen Gebäudes zeigt sich nur nach vorurteilsloser Analyse.

Den strukturellen und masslichen Eigenheiten des Baus und der Vielfalt des Raumprogramms wird mit einer klaren, neuen Erschliessungsfigur begegnet und durch deren Variation gleichzeitig die Differenzierung und Identität der drei umgebauten Geschosse gewonnen. Die «Wavy Horizontal Bands with Colors Superimposed», die Sol LeWitt für die ihm vorgegebenen architektonischen Situationen eigens geschaffen hat, unterstützen die räumliche Strategie der Architekten und werden selbstverständlicher Bestandteil. Nicht zuletzt entsteht ein Spannungsbogen über die ganze Orientierungsfigur: So zeigt die hell leuchtende Glasbausteinwand am einen Ende jedes Korridors die Himmelsrichtung an, während die Wellen am anderen Ende auf dem gegenläufigen Korridor verweisen und mit ihrer unterschiedlichen Farbigkeit dem Ortsgedächtnis seine eigene Schattierung einprägen.

Zurich's commercial buildings constructed in the 60s and 70s are likely to remain a functioning element of the city for a long time. The original strong demand for flexible use, which resulted in the structural distinction between the load-bearing structure and interior elements, now presents an opportunity to revitalise the torsos from the inside. The pragmatic floor plan, some of which is partially tripartite and partially tends towards an open matrix, is open to several interpretations. The implied windmill form is the result of attempting to optimise both its function (cubicle offices/group rooms) and the building volume within the plot and estate, rather than design intentions. The building is air-conditioned and the floor heights are minimised. The interior work no longer fulfils today's (technical, fire safety, organisational and design) standards. The performance potential of such a building can only be revealed through an unprejudiced analysis.

The structural and dimensional qualities of the building and the diversity of the spatial programme is met with a clear, new distribution figure. Its variation helps to achieve the distinction and identity of the three converted floors. The "Wavy Horizontal Bands with Colors Superimposed", which were specifically created by Sol Le Witt for the given architectural situations, support the spatial strategy of the architects and become naturally integrated elements. Equally important suspense is generated over the entire orientation figure: the brightly illuminated glass block wall at one end of each corridor indicates the compass direction, while the waves at the other end indicate the opposing corridor, their different colours and distinct tones etching a specific shade into the memory of the place.

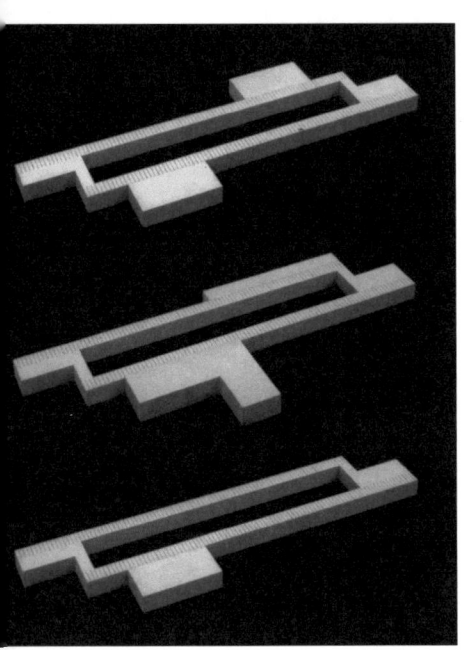

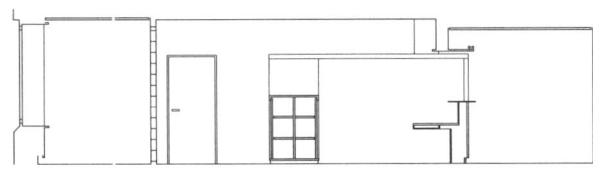

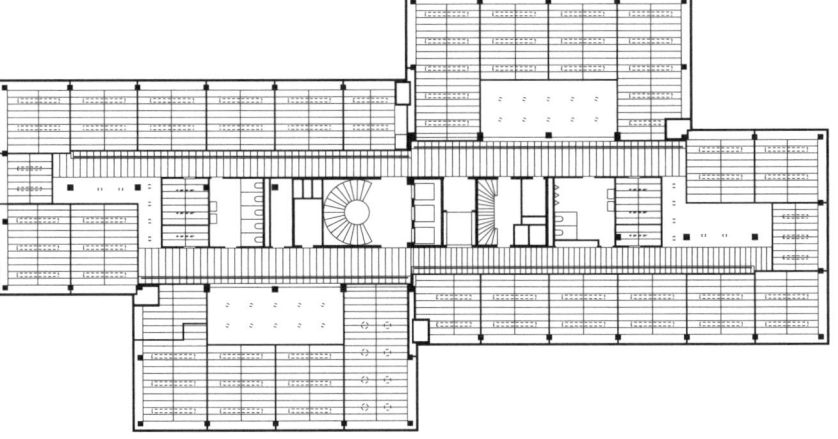

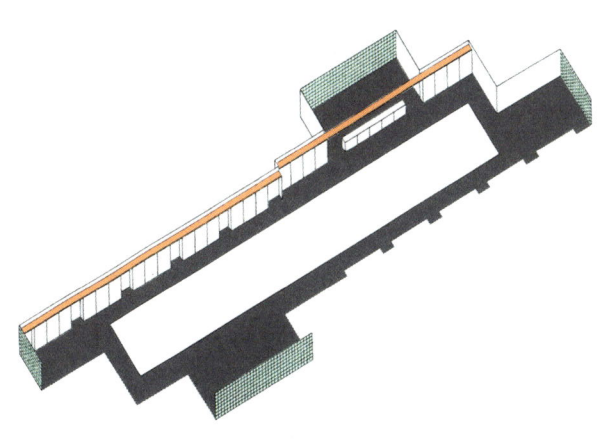

Instandsetzung Verwaltungsgebäude, Niederurnen

Renovation of an administration building, Niederurnen

Baujahr / Year of construction:
1954–1955, 1964
Architekten / Architects: Haefeli Moser Steiger, Zürich
Direktauftrag / Direct commission: 1997
Ausführung / Construction measure:
1998–2005 (in Etappen / in stages)
Auftraggeber / Client: Eternit Schweiz

Die erste wesentliche Veränderung erfährt das Gebäude 1964 durch die Erweiterung. Erst wenn man davon weiss und entsprechend sucht, wird sie sichtbar. So wenig zum Stichwort «Weiterbauen». Seither findet nichts Aussergewöhnliches statt: Eine Vielzahl scheinbar harmloser Anpassungen im Innern, der alltägliche Pragmatismus, führt zur üblichen schleichenden Veränderung. Dabei verschwinden markante Teile: die abgehängten Decken aus perforiertem Welleternit in den Korridoren, die skulpturale Anlage für die Warmluftheizung im Ausstellungstrakt und vieles mehr.

Der heutige Nutzer und Bauherr kennt die Bedeutung seines Hauses als Demonstrationsobjekt, als authentischen Zeugen der damaligen Eternit-Technologie und als Werk bedeutender Architekten. Spuren des Gebrauchs sind zugelassen, das Altern ist sichtbar und vieles hat zu einer eigenen Schönheit gefunden. Das Verständnis des Bauherrn für sein Haus ist die Voraussetzung für die seit 1997 durch uns erfolgten Arbeiten.

Büros: prototypische Sanierung mit neuen Leuchten und Eternit-Tischen. Empfang: Umbau, technische Aufrüstung. Postanlieferung: neue Treppe. WC-Anlagen im Erweiterungsbau: Sanierung und ein neues Behinderten-WC. Ausstellungstrakt: etappenweise Fensterreparatur mit gleichwertigem Ersatz der transparenten Wärmedämmung. Gebäudehülle: Studie zum Energiehaushalt mit dem Resultat, dass das komplexe Eternit-Kleid geschont werden kann. Farbanalysen. Fassaden: Unterhalt und Reparatur der West- und Nordseite, energetische Verbesserung der alten Holzfenster. Windfang: Einbau von automatischen Schiebetüren, Handläufe für die Eingänge. Dach: Dämmung und Neueindeckung.

In diesem wohldurchdachten Gefüge von Haefeli Moser Steiger wird jegliche angestrengte Didaktik vermieden, welche Alt und Neu polarisiert: die Interventionen sind sozusagen «unsichtbar».

The building underwent its first significant conversion in 1964, when it was extended. Only those who know that fact and seek it will discover its traces. So much for the subject subject of "continued building". Since then, nothing unusual has happened: a large number of apparently harmless adaptations to the interior, everyday pragmatism, have led to the usual creeping transformation. Striking elements disappear in this way: the suspended ceilings made of perforated, corrugated Eternit in the corridors, the sculptural equipment for the warm air heating in the exhibition wing and much more.

The current user and contractor is aware of the significance of the building as a as a prestigious object object, an authentic witness of the Eternit technology of the time and as a work by significant architects. Traces of use are permitted, aging is visible and much has developed its own beauty with time. The contractor's awareness of his building is the precondition for the work carried out since 1997.

Offices: prototype renovation with new lighting and Eternit tables. Lobby area: conversion and technical improvement. Post delivery area: new stairs. Toilet facilities: renovation plus a new toilet for the disabled. Exhibition wing: gradual window repairs including an equivalent replacement of the transparent insulation panels between the glass panes. Building shell: study on the energy budget, with the result of preserving the complex Eternit "dress". Colour analyses. Façades: maintenance and repair of the west and north façades, energy improvements to the old wooden windows. Vestibule: installation of automatic sliding doors, hand railings for the entrances. Roof: insulation and new roofing.

In this well-conceived structure by Haefeli Moser Steiger, any strained didactics that would polarise old and new are avoided: The interventions are quasi "invisible".

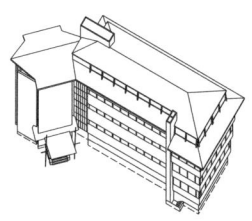 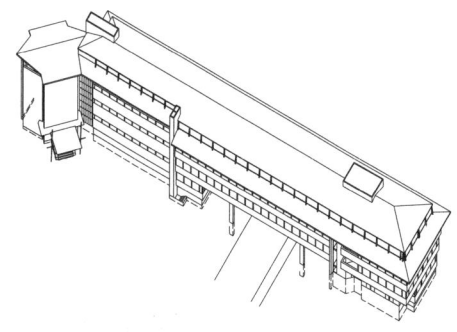 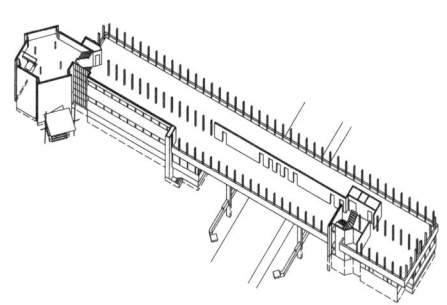

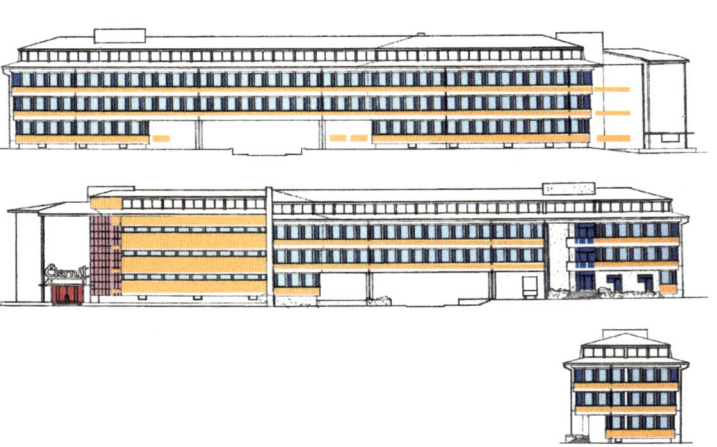

Sanierung Dach

Dach

Sanierung WC

Dachgeschoss   **Teilsanierung Büros**

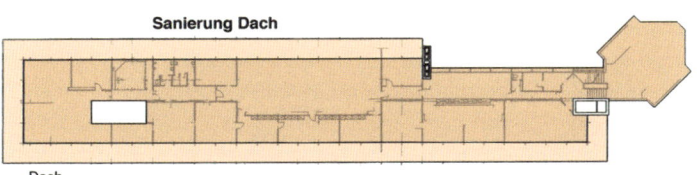

2. Obergeschoss   **Prototyp Sanierung Büros**

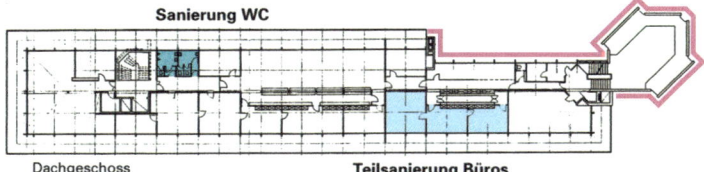

Sanierung Gebäudehülle   Neubau 1964 ★ Altbau 1955

1. Obergeschoss

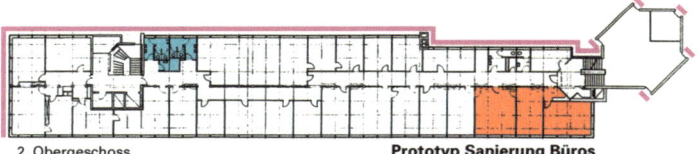

Sanierung Windfang

Sanierung Postanlieferung

Sanierung Empfang

Erdgeschoss

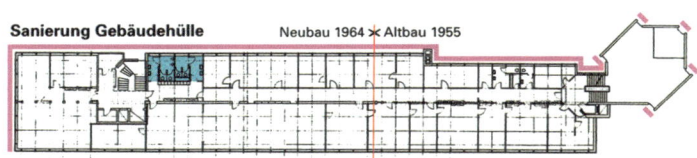
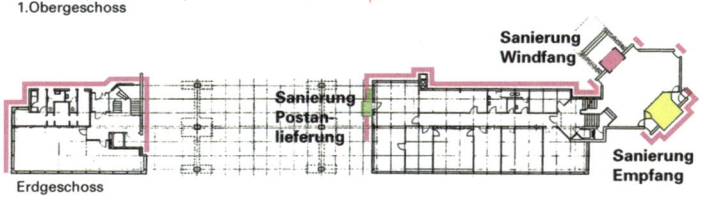

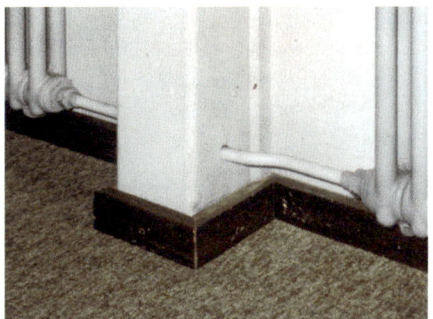 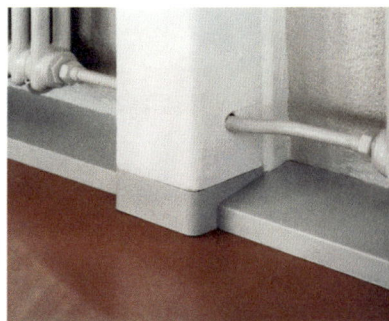

Umbau und Instandsetzung Amtshaus III, Zürich

Conversion and repair of Amtshaus III administration building, Zurich

Baujahr / Year of construction: 1914
Architekt / Architect: Gustav Gull, Zürich
Direktauftrag / Direct commission: 1997
Ausführung / Construction measure: 1998–2004, 2009–2011 (in 7 Etappen / 7 stages)
Auftraggeber / Client: Amt für Hochbauten der Stadt Zürich / City of Zurich Construction Authority (Peter Ess)

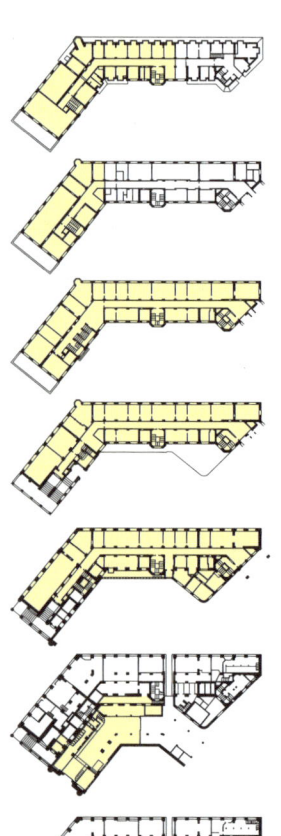

Das Amtshaus III von Gustav Gull gehört zu seinen bescheideneren öffentlichen Bauten. Bemerkenswert sind die Treppenanlagen, die von solider Schreinerarbeit geprägten Korridore und die auch hier souveräne Lichtführung. Zu erwähnen sind aber auch die vielen im Laufe der Jahre erfolgten Veränderungen. Der Bau soll im Rahmen seiner Leistungsfähigkeit für eine moderne Verwaltung respektvoll erneuert werden: Der Bauherr wünscht technische Aufrüstung, Anpassung des Brandschutzes und eine offene, kommunikative Arbeitsweise unter den Mitarbeitern auch mithilfe baulicher Mittel.

Welche Sprache sollen die neuen Architekten hier sprechen? Die Authentizität von Gulls Architektur liegt in ihrer Substanz, aber auch in der inneren Logik, im Katalog von Regeln, welche die Verhältnisse – auch die Mengenverhältnisse – ordnen. Ein Verändern derselben führt u. U. zu dem Moment, wo die kritische Masse unterschritten wird und somit die architektonische Identität kippt. Die Sorge darum generiert folgende Spielregeln: 1. Die gullsche Identität ist zu stärken. 2. Für jede Frage ist die Antwort zuerst im gullschen Katalog der Elemente und Regeln zu suchen. 3. Ergibt Punkt 2 keine Antwort, so ist sie aus der gullschen inneren Logik zu entwickeln. Ausnahmen erfordern Argumente. 4. Jede Frage ist nach diesen Spielregeln abzuwickeln. Gestalterische Automatismen und Klischees sind zu unterlassen. 5. Der Zweifel sei treuer Begleiter.

Diskret selbstbewusst helfen Neuerungen wie eigens entwickelte Deckenleuchten und Akustikmassnahmen, in einem «Deckenrelief» zusammengefasst, Schalter und Steckdosen, Bodenkanal/Sockel, Bodenbeläge (Büros und Korridore differenziert), Büroverbindungen mit alubelegten Schiebepaneelen und grossflächige Stoffrollos die bewährte gullsche Räumlichkeit atmosphärisch anzureichern und mit neuer Deutlichkeit zu zeichnen.

The Amtshaus III is one of Gustav Gull's more unobtrusive public buildings. The staircases, the corridors characterised by fine carpentry and the skilful light guidance are all remarkable. The many changes made over the years should also be mentioned. The building was to be respectfully renewed within its potential to allow modern administration: the client demands technical enhancements, adapted fire protection and – supported by means of architecture – an open, communicative working atmosphere for the staff.

Which language should the new architects speak? The authenticity of Gull's architecture lies in its substance, as well as its inner logic, the catalogue of rules that order the relationships as well as proportions. Changing them can lead to the moment where the critical mass is undercut, at which point the architectural identity collapses. This concern leads to the following rules of the game: 1. Gull's identity should be strengthened. 2. The answer to every question should initially be sought in Gull's catalogue of elements and rules. 3. If 2. provides no solution, it should be developed using Gull's inner logic. 4. Each question must be handled using these rules. Design automatisms and clichés must be avoided. Exceptions require arguments. 5. Doubt should be a constant companion.

Discreetly confident amendments such as the specially developed ceiling lighting and acoustic measures that are integrated into a "ceiling relief", switches and sockets, ground cabling/bases, flooring (that distinguish the offices and the corridors), office connections with aluminium-covered sliding panels and large-scale fabric roller blinds enrich Gull's trusted spatial atmosphere and give it a new clarity.

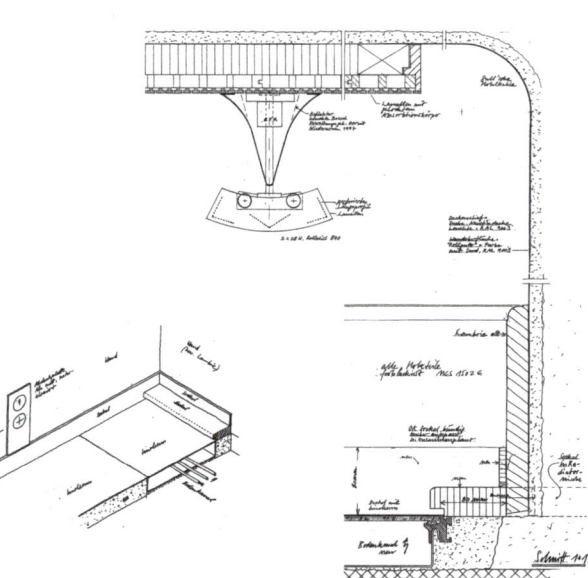

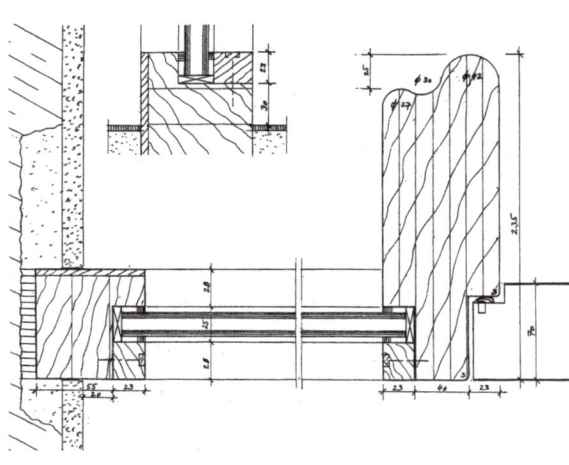

Umbau Werkhof Uraniastrasse, Zürich

Maintenance depot conversion, Uraniastrasse, Zurich

Baujahr / Year of construction: 1914
Architekt / Architect: Gustav Gull, Zürich
Direktauftrag / Direct commission: 2003
Ausführung / Construction measure: 2003–2005
Auftraggeber / Client: Amt für Hochbauten der Stadt Zürich / City of Zurich Construction Authority (Peter Ess)

Die Brücke über die Uraniastrasse ist Teil von Gustav Gulls Projekt für die Amtshäuser. Der in der Pfeilerhalle im nördlichen Brückenkopf untergebrachte Werkhof war bezüglich Hygiene, technischer Ausrüstung und Sicherheit seit Langem eine Zumutung.

Die Halle wird bis auf die Tragstruktur ausgeräumt und neu ausgebaut. Die bestehenden Konsolen an den Betonpfeilern werden zum Auflagern von neuen Decken und einer Verbindungsgalerie mit Brücke reaktiviert. Im Obergeschoss sind die Stützenfelder mit Glasbaustein ausgefacht. Dem ruppigen Betrieb entspricht die robust-rohe Halle und mehrschichtige Kleidung schützt die Arbeiter. Dort, wo diese verletzlicher sind, in der Garderobe und der Dusche aber auch im Aufenthalts-/Essraum auf dem Galeriegeschoss, entspricht der Ausbaustandard demjenigen des angrenzenden Amtshauses III.

Wo sich *white collar* und *blue collar* tatsächlich näher kommen, ist am kleinen Lichthof, an der Schnittstelle beider Bauten. Mit Gefängniszellen zugebaut, musste er erst entdeckt, befreit und neu interpretiert werden. Der Zauber dieses kleinen Raumes entfaltet sich, wo niemand Derartiges erwartet hätte. Der Ort – flankiert von die zwei Pausenräumen – hat seine eigene Farbigkeit. Und er beschenkt diese, welche sich im wohltemperierten Büro sitzend um die städtischen Bauten kümmern, gleichermassen wie jene, die sich bei jedem Wetter um den von uns auf den Strassen zurückgelassenen Schmutz und Müll kümmern.

Und die zwei Schlangenköpfe? Vom Schlosser mit wenig Aufwand und einiger Freude hergestellt, befinden sie sich dort, wo das Geländer der inneren Brücke Fragen aufwirft, und sind eine Reverenz an Dutzende von geschmiedeten Schlangen, welche die Kellerfenster am benachbarten Amtshaus I schützen.

The bridge over Uraniastrasse is part of Gustav Gull's project for the municipal administration buildings. The maintenance depot situated in the pillared hall inside the northern bridgehead had long been in a very poor condition in terms of hygiene, technical equipment and safety.

The hall was stripped down to its load bearing structure and converted. The existing brackets on the concrete pillars were reactivated to support new ceilings and a connecting gallery with a flyover bridge. On the gallery floor, the spans between the columns are filled in using glass blocks. The robust, raw hall befits the rough operation mode, and multilayered cladding protects the workers. Where they are more vulnerable, in the changing rooms, showers and in the recreation room on the gallery level, the finishing standard corresponds with the neighbouring Amtshaus III.

Where *white collar* and *blue collar* workers actually come close to each other, there is a small inner courtyard at the intersection between the two buildings. Formerly closed in by prison cells, it had first to be discovered, freed and newly interpreted. The magic of this small space unfolds where no-one had expected it. The place – flanked by two recreation rooms – has its own colour tone, which radiates towards people sitting in their well-conditioned offices of the municipal building, as well as those who deal in all kinds of weather with the dirt and rubbish we leave behind on the streets.

What of the two snake's heads? Produced by the locksmith with a little effort and much joy, they are situated where the railings of the inner flyover bridge raise questions and are a reference to the dozens of crafted snakes that protect the cellar windows of the neighbouring Amtshaus I.

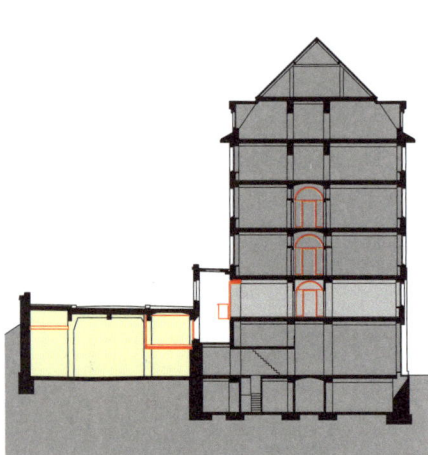

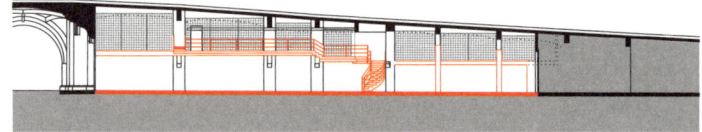

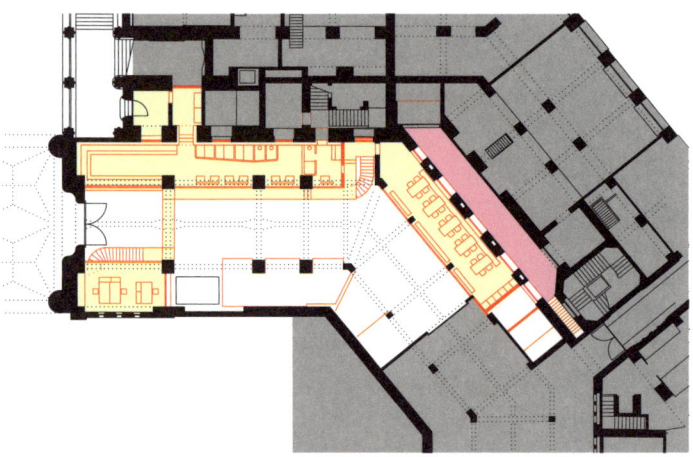

Begegnungszentrum, psychiatrische Klinik, Königsfelden

Meeting centre, Königsfelden Psychiatric Clinic

Wettbewerb / Competition: 1997
Auftraggeber / Client: Psychiatrische Klinik, Königsfelden / Königsfelden Psychiatric Clinic

Auf dem Hinweg signalisiert das Rot, das zwischen den Bäumen aufscheint, für die Dauer eines kurzen Wegstückes das Ziel. Zwei Hauptelemente, die Wandelhalle und die «Häuser», machen das neue Begegnungszentrum aus. Das «öffentliche» Element: ein Bau aus Holz, der die angenehmen Eigenschaften von vertrauten Architekturen aufweist, von der Wandelhalle, der Laube, dem Wintergarten, dem Portikus, der Stoa oder auch der Veranda; zuvorderst – am Ort des alten Kioskes – schätzt man die Eigenschaften der gedeckten Gartenterrasse. Das Angebot der Wandelhalle für den Gebrauch ist vielfältig und reich: im Alltag ebenso wie bei besonderen Gelegenheiten, bei Feiern und Festen. Auch an trüben, nassen und kalten Tagen ist sie ein Ort, wo man sich ohne Verpflichtung aufhalten kann, mit anderen zusammen oder auch für sich, ohne allein zu sein. Abends kann man Vorhänge ziehen, der Bau scheint dann von aussen gleich einer schimmernden Laterne.

Zur ruhigen Gartenseite hin, in robust-einfacher Bauweise und übersichtlich angeordnet, liegen die einzelnen «Häuser», die den enger umschriebenen Nutzungen Raum geben (Kiosk, Café, Klubräume, Cheminéezimmer, Treppe, Besprechungsräume, Bibliothek). Proportionierung, Material, Zeichnung des Bodens und sorgfältige Farbgebung verleihen den «Häusern» ihren stimmungsvoll-ruhigen Charakter und vermitteln Geborgenheit. Wie die anderen «Häuser» öffnet sich auch das Cheminéezimmer mit grossen Fenstern zum Garten hin.

Nebeneinander und ohne ihr Gespräch zu unterbrechen, können zwei Personen die breit und bequem flach angelegte Treppe begehen, die in einem lichten und hellen Raum in den oberen Stock führt. 5 m über dem Boden befreit sich die Sicht. Gerichtet wie eine Kompassnadel ruht der intime Bibliotheksraum in der Weite der Landschaft.

Bürointern wie -extern erwies sich das Projekt – eine lapidar einfache Anordnung – als anregend.

Moving towards the meeting centre, the red that appears between the trees indicates the destination for a brief moment. Two main elements, the "Wandelhalle" and the "houses", characterise the new encounter centre. The "public" element is a wooden structure with agreeable qualities of familiar architecture, such as the foyer, the gazebo, the winter garden, the portico, the stoa and also the veranda. At the front – where the old kiosk used to be – the qualities of the covered garden terrace are especially appreciated. The range of possibilities of the "Wandelhalle" is diverse and rich: both in everyday situations and on special occasions, such as celebrations and festivities. Even on grey, wet and cold days, it remains a place to linger without compulsion, meet others or remain alone. In the evenings, the curtains can be drawn, making the building appear from the outside like a glimmering lantern.

Towards the quiet garden side, in a robustly simple construction aligned in a clear way, the individual "houses" provide space for the uses described in detail (kiosk, café, club rooms, fireside room, stairs, library). The proportions, materials, floor design and careful colouring give the "houses" their atmospheric character and communicate a sense of security. Like the other types of "houses", the fireside room's large windows open out into the garden.

Without needing to interrupt their conversation, two people can simultaneously use the broad, comfortable stairs that lead to a light, bright room on the upper storey. The view unfolds five metres above the ground. Aligned like a compass needle, the intimate library rests in the broad expanse of the landscape. Both within and outside our office, the project's succinct, simple order proved to be inspirational.

Schloss Chillon

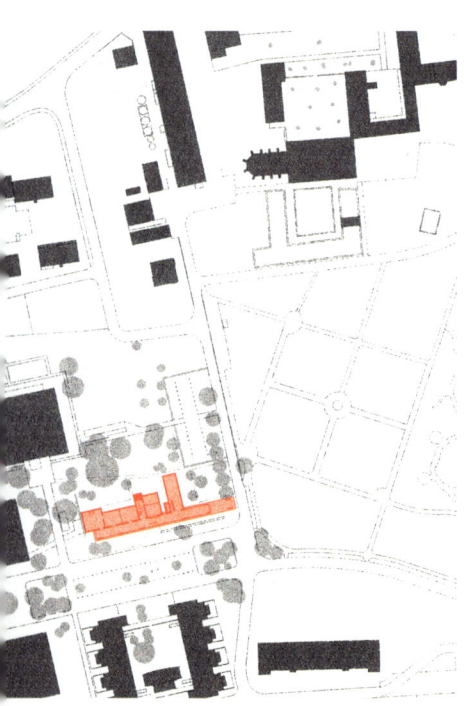

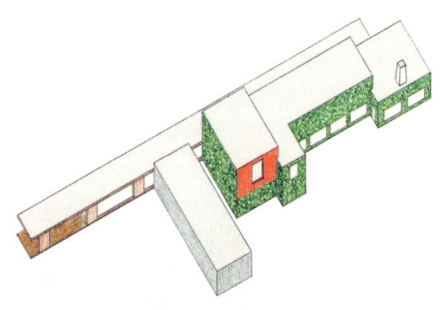

Kindergarten, Mollis

Wettbewerb / Competition: 2005
Bauingenieur / Civil engineer:
Walt + Galmarini, Zürich
Aussenraumgestaltung / Landscape design: Jane Sörensen, Hamburg
Auftraggeber / Client: Gemeinde Mollis, Glarus Nord

Auf dem bergseitigen Ufer des ehemaligen Industriekanales stehen mit schweren Sockeln fest im Boden verankerte Gebäude, während die Holzkonstruktion des Kindergartens aufgeständert über der Ebene liegt. Einem Floss gleich scheint der niedrige, flächige Bau auf dem feuchten Schwemmland vertäut. Vergleichbar mit dem Projekt in Königsfelden sind einem gemeinschaftlichen «grossen» Hauptraum – sozusagen ein Stück Strasse – die Gruppenräume angegliedert – sozusagen die Häuser der Kinder – mit eigener Infrastruktur, einer kleinen Galerie, einem Erker und bergendem Dach. Zusammen mit dem Vordach über dem schützenden Umgang, der als *space inbetween,* ringsum laufende äussere Verbindung und lange Bank zum Garten hin gelesen werden kann, wird dieses als räumliches Faltwerk statisch wirksam. Eine umlaufende gelochte Blende legt den inneren Horizont tief und leitet den Blick auf das Wasser des Kanals, und das Grün der Wiesenflächen und die Stämme des Obstgartens der äusseren Landschaft. Der Geruch und der Klang des Holzes, seine optischen und haptischen Eigenheiten, bestimmen atmosphärisch die innere Landschaft. Das Preisgericht bevorzugte klassische Kammlösungen.

Buildings with heavy foundations firmly anchored into the ground are situated on the hillside bank of the former industrial canal, while the wooden structure of the kindergarten is floor-mounted and lies above the plain. Like a raft, the low, spacious building seems to be moored on the damp alluvial soil. In a similar way to the project in Königsfelden, the group rooms are aligned along a common "large" main room, like a section of a street – the children's houses as it were – with their own infrastructure, a small gallery, a bay window and the large protecting roof. Together with the canopy covering the walkway, which can be interpreted as a space in between, an enveloping outer connection and a long bench to the garden, the folded roof construction becomes spatially effective. A surrounding perforated blind lays the inner horizon low and guides the view to the water of the canal, the green meadows and the trunks of the orchard in the surrounding countryside. The scent and sound of the wood, its optic and haptic qualities, atmospherically define the inner landscape. The competition jury preferred traditional ridge solutions.

Søllerød, Arne Jacobsen, 1942

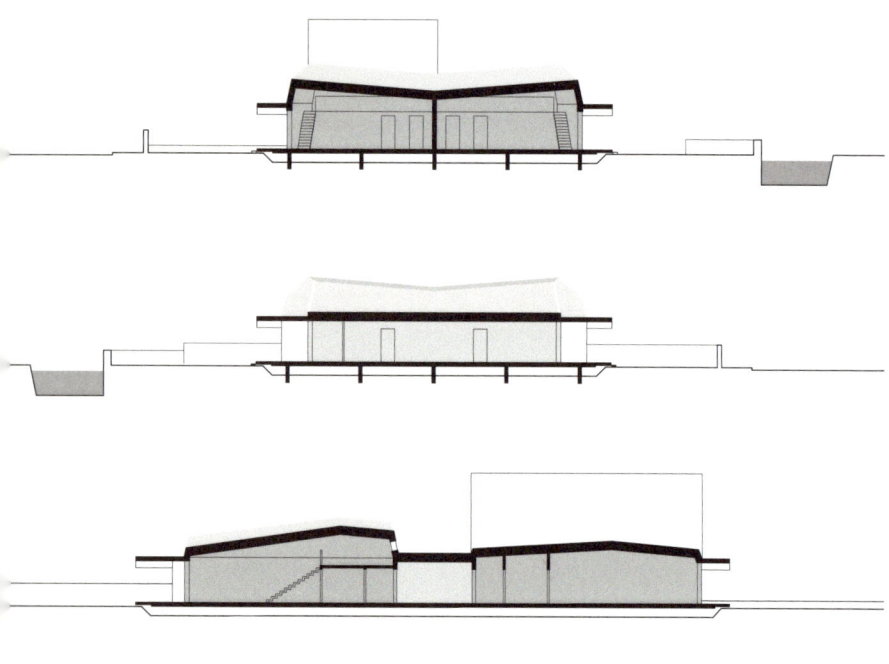

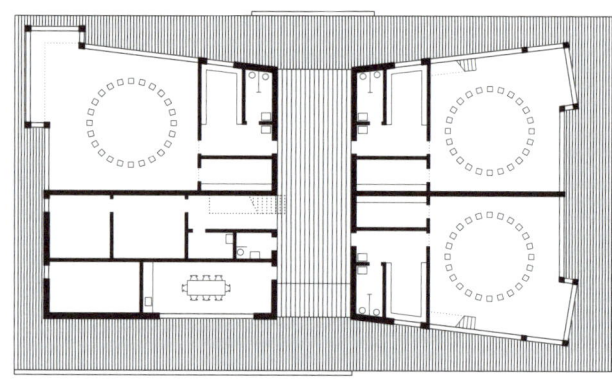

Instandsetzung Haus Kind, Riehen

Renovation, Kind house, Riehen

Baujahr / Year of construction: 1930
Architekt / Architect: Bräuning Leu, Basel
Direktauftrag / Direct commission: 2006
Ausführung / Construction measure: 2007–2008
Bauphysik / Structural physics: BWS, Winterthur
Auftraggeber / Client: privat / private

Das Haus für die Künstlerin Brunhilde Kind wurde an der Geländekante eines Osthanges weit ausserhalb des Dorfes, aber in Sichtdistanz zweier Häuser, von Artaria & Schmidt erbaut. Im Erdgeschoss sind ein 4 m hohes Atelier mit Oberlicht und genordetem Atelierfenster und ein 3 m hohes Atelier, welches mit Oberlicht und geostetem Atelierfenster sowie der Farbgebung (Wände/Decke neapelgelb, Holzzementboden rot, Holzwerk/Metallfenster dunkelblau) wohl eher als Salon mit der Anmutung eines Ateliers gedacht und gelebt war.

Darunter liegen die kleine neapelgelbe Küche und das blaue Privatzimmer mit gelben Türen zum orangenen Bad bzw. zum Garten, bergseitig ein Kellerraum.

Der Bau wurde fast ohne Unterbruch bewohnt, unterhalten und als Atelierhaus genutzt. Konstruktionsbedingte Schwachstellen, Abnutzung und altersbedingte Schäden machten Instandsetzungen und Erneuerungen nötig: Oberlichter, Rostsanierungen an Stahlträgern und Fensterstürzen, Elektro- und Sanitärinstallationen, innere und äussere Oberflächen. Der einfache Ausbaustandard und Ergänzungen aus den 1940er-Jahren, welche den Gebrauchswert und Komfort dauerhaft verbessert hatten, wurden beibehalten (Vorfenster, Windfangtüre, Küchentüre, Galerie), die ehemalige Polychromie wieder hergestellt.

Der mit zementösen Flicken durchsetzte alte Putz wurde repariert und mit einem dünnen Kalkputz in der Farbe trockener Erde überzogen. Das erstmalige Dämmen der Dächer, Kellerdecken, eines unerwarteten Wandhohlraumes sowie zweier gefährdeter Aussenwände (mineralischer Dämmputz) senkten den Ölverbrauch markant und erhöhten den Komfort in bis dahin klimatisch problematischen Räumen. Mit dem Versetzen der zur Strasse orientierten, hohen Ateliertür wurde vom Konzept der sanften Sanierung abgewichen: Dem Ateliergeschoss erschliesst sich neu der Garten. Seit 2008 steht das Haus unter Denkmalschutz.

The house for the artist Brunhilde Kind was built on a ridge of an eastern slope, far outside the village, but within sight of two buildings by Artaria/Schmidt. On the ground floor, there is a 4 m high studio with a skylight and a north-facing studio window and a 3 m high studio, which has a skylight and an east-facing studio window. The colours of the smaller studio (walls/ceilings in Naples yellow, woodwork/metal windows in dark blue, floor in brick-red) reflect its conception and use more as a salon with the feel of a studio.

Beneath it is a small Naples yellow kitchen and the blue private room with yellow doors leading to the orange-red bathroom and the garden.

The building has been inhabited, maintained and used as a studio almost without interruption. Structural weak points, wear and age-related damage made maintenance and renovation necessary: skylights, rust repair to the steel girders and window lintels, electrical and sanitary installations, inner and outer surfaces. The simple standard of finishing and additions made in the 40s, which provided a long-term improvement in the use value and made the house more comfortable, were retained (additional external windows, porch door, kitchen door, gallery), while the former polychromy was restored.

The old plaster that had been patched with cement was repaired and covered with a thin layer of lime plaster in the colour of dry earth. The first-time insulation of the roofs, cellar ceilings, an unexpected wall cavity and two endangered exterior walls (mineral insulation plaster) significantly reduced oil consumption and made the rooms that were previously climatically problematic more comfortable. Moving the high studio door facing the street meant a slight divergence from the concept of gentle renovation: the studio floor now has an access to the garden. The building has been preservation-listed since 2008.

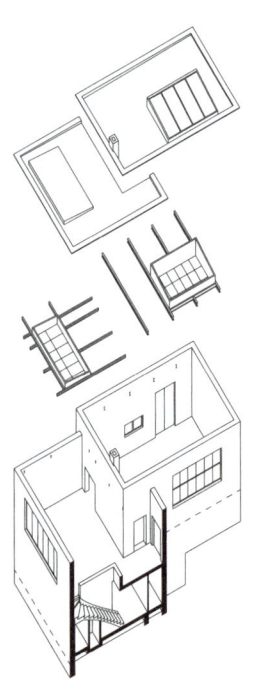

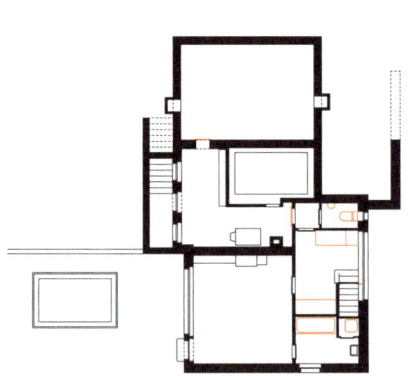

Wohnhaus S-M, Zürich
S-M residential building, Zurich

Baujahr / Year of construction: 1920
Direktauftrag / Direct commission: 2003
Ausführung / Construction measure:
2003–2004
Bauingenieur / Civil engineer:
APT Ingenieure, Zürich
Auftraggeber / Client: privat / private

Das dreigeschossige Haus soll für eine Familie instand gesetzt werden. In seinem Ausdruck ein Nachfahre der Reformarchitektur, wurde es vor der Erfindung der Freizeit erbaut. Der Garten diente der Selbstversorgung. Ein direkter Zugang war nicht nötig. Und der Architekt ersparte sich das Eingehen auf die Hanglage, das Haus war eingesichtig. Das Wohn- und Schlafgeschoss weist Zimmer von 10, 14 und 21 m^2 auf. Ihre handlichen Fenster sind nur so gross, dass der Bewohner nicht der bedrängenden Schönheit und Präsenz der äusseren Landschaft ausgesetzt ist. Der Ausblick in diese ist wunderbar, wohldosiert und ganz nebenbei.

Das Wohngeschoss erfährt mit dem Anbau eine bedeutende Ausweitung. Sein offener Raum findet sich aufgehoben in der Intimität des neu erschlossenen Gartens hinter dem Haus. Das Fünfeck verdankt seine unregelmässige Form der Ausrichtung des Blickes in überraschende Tiefen des neu entdeckten Hinterlandes, dem Grenzverlauf sowie dem räumlichen Verhältnis zwischen Esstisch und Glaswänden. Die grösstmögliche Verglasung ist nicht per se gut. Ihrer räumlichen Unbestimmtheit wirken Stellung, Form und Sockel der Stützen, Vorhang, Rankgitter, Kletterpflanzen, Dachvorsprung, Plattenumgang und Sitzmauer entgegen und schaffen einen Übergang. Das Koordinatennetz von Travertinintarsien im Terrazzo verbindet mit der Geometrie des Hauses.

Die schlichte Schönheit, die dem Inneren dieses etwas biederen Hauses eigen ist, bedurfte nur der achtsamen Hilfestellung der Architekten, ohne hinzuzufügen, ohne wegzunehmen: Es waren Glücksmomente, als Zimmer und Treppe ihr stilles Leuchten wiedergewannen.

Wann ist ein Haus fertig? Das Äussere des Anbaus besteht sozusagen nur aus einem angedeuteten Aufriss: Zwei gefaltete und um 45° gedrehte Armierungsnetze mit fensterartiger Auslassung sowie die Hege und Pflege durch die Bewohner helfen Wein- und Waldrebe beim Zeichnen und Verfertigen der Fassaden.

A family asks to overhaul their three-storey house. A descendant of reform architecture in terms of its expression, it was constructed before the invention of leisure. The garden was used for self-sufficiency. Direct access was not required. And the architect refrained from dealing with the sloping terrain so the house only has one main front. The living and bedroom floor has rooms with sizes of 10, 14 and 21 m^2. Their convenient windows are small enough to prevent the inhabitant from being exposed to the impressive beauty and presence of the outside landscape. The view into it is wonderful, measured and very relaxed.

The living area has been significantly enlarged by the extension. Its open space is accommodated in the intimacy of the newly accessed garden behind the house. The pentagon has its irregular shape due to the alignment of the view into the surprising depths of the newly discovered hinterland, the line of the property boundary and the spatial relationship between the dining table and the glass walls. The largest possible amount of glass is not always good per se. Its indefinite spatial nature is counteracted by the position, form and base of the wooden columns, curtain, creeper trellis, climbing plants, projecting roof, paved walkway and concrete bench, so transition is created. The coordinate frame of travertine inlay in the terrazzo floor connects with the geometry of the house.

The unpretentious beauty in this rather modest house only required the architects' careful support, without addition or removal: there were moments of happiness when the rooms and stairway regained their silent radiance.

When is a house finished? The exterior of the extension almost exclusively consists of an implied elevation: two folded reinforcement nets that are rotated by 45° with window-like openings, as well as the residents' care, help the vine and clematis delineate and finish the façades.

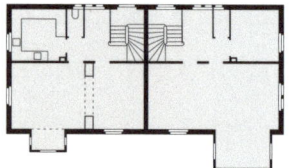

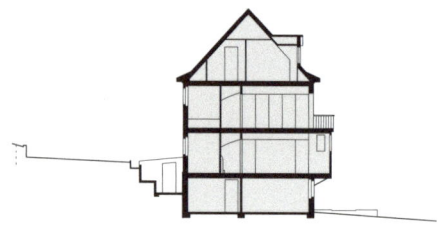

Vorher / Before

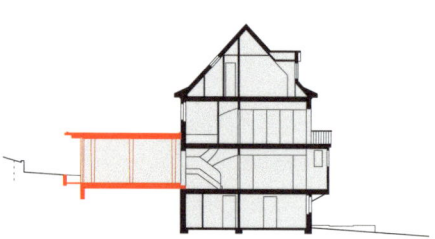

Nachher / After

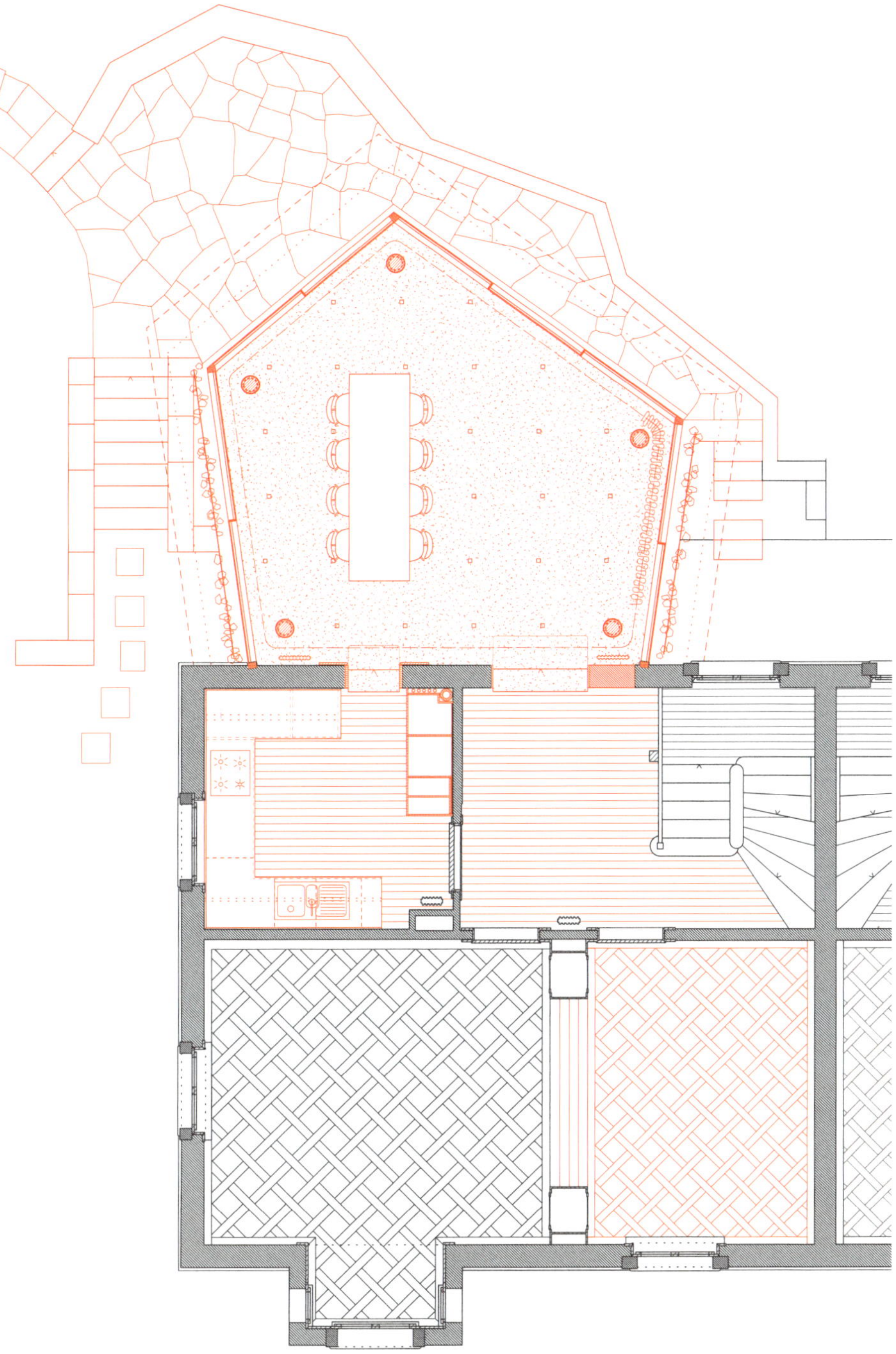

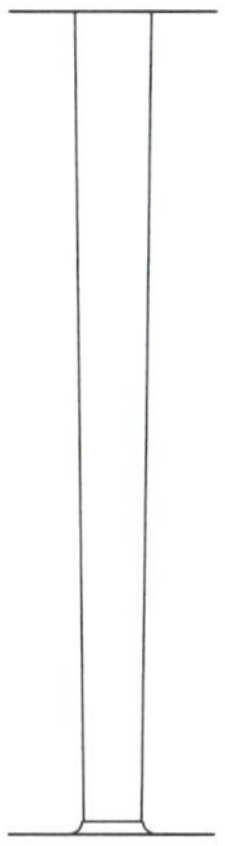

Gartenhalle, Gartenhaus, Berneck

Garden hall and summerhouse, Berneck

Direktauftrag / Direct commission: 2006
Ausführung / Construction measure: 2007–2008
Auftraggeber / Client: privat / private

Die Gartenhalle ergänzt das bestehende Wohn- und Werkstattgebäude und begrenzt den Garten zur Strasse. Der kleine Bau mit Kamin, kleiner Küche und Nasszelle besteht aus einer Holzkonstruktion auf einer Betonplatte. Das Dachprofil verschleiert mehr, als dass es erklärt, es verbirgt den Fachwerkträger zur Überspannung der grossen Öffnung. Strassen- und Gartenseite unterscheiden sich deutlich: mit einem geschlossenen, hellgrau gestrichenen, rauen Schindelpanzer und einer glatten graublauen Täfelung auf Wand und Decke, die sich vom Äussern ins Innere einstülpt. Wenn die grossen verglasten Schiebetüren in die Wände eingefahren sind, sitzt man tatsächlich in einer Gartenhalle, d.h. zwar draussen, aber durch Wände und Dach geschützt. Sind die Schiebetüren geschlossen, wird das Innere zum reinen Innenraum mit seinem eigenen Schwerpunkt. Ein Vorhang erhöht die Wandelbarkeit. Kleine Variationen im Regelhaften, wie gesondert zugeschnittene Einsprengsel im Schindelpanzer oder eine Reihe von durchbohrten Schindeln an der Kante des Vordachs, durchbrochene Täferbretter vor den Heizkörpern, aber auch eine Intarsie aus Schieferplatten in der Kieselzeichnung des geschliffenen Betonbodens, verweisen auf die traditionelle Neigung zum Schmücken. Diese Art von Schmuck hat immer auch eine Aufgabe. Und ist Stoff für Missverständnisse zwischen dem Städter und dem Dorfbewohner.

The garden hall supplements the existing residential and workshop building and limits the garden towards the street. The small building with a fireside, a small kitchen and a bathroom module consists of a wooden structure on a concrete base. The roof profile veils more than it explains; it conceals the timber beams to span the large opening.
The street and garden sides differ strongly: with a closed, coarse shingle shell painted in light grey on the street side, while on the garden side, there is smooth grey panelling on the walls and ceilings, which folds inwards from the outside. When the large glass sliding doors are stowed away into the walls, one actually sits in a garden hall, i.e. outside, but protected by walls and roof. If the siding doors are closed, the inside becomes pure interior space with its own inner focus. A curtain increases the transformability. Minor variations in the set of rules, such as specifically tailored interspersions in the shingle shell, as well as a series of perforated shingles at the edge of the projecting roof, pierced panels in front of the radiators and also an inlay made of slate plates in the pebble design of the polished concrete floor, are all references to the traditional tendency towards decoration. This type of decorative element always also has a task – and is providing material for misunderstandings, between townsfolk and villagefolk.

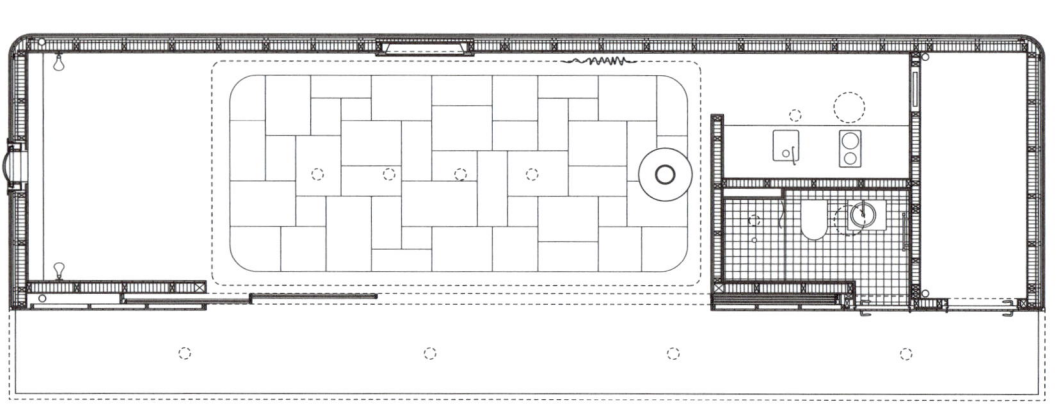
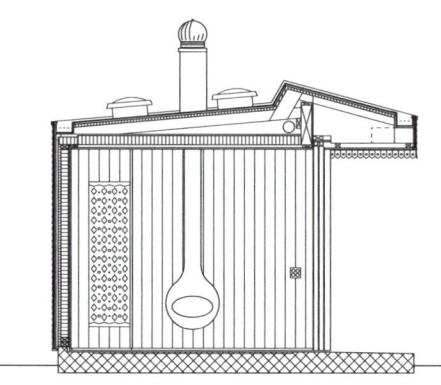

Pavillon Oui!, expo.02, Yverdon-les-Bains

Direktauftrag / Direct commission: 2001
Ausführung / Construction measure: 2001–2002
Demontage / Dismantled: 2002
Bauingenieur / Civil engineer: Walt + Galmarini, Zürich
Haustechnik / Building equipment: Ernst Basler + Partner, Zürich
Auftraggeber / Client: expo.02

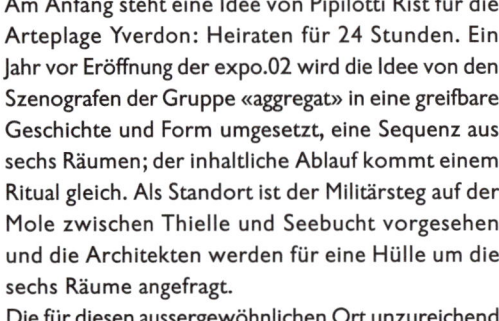

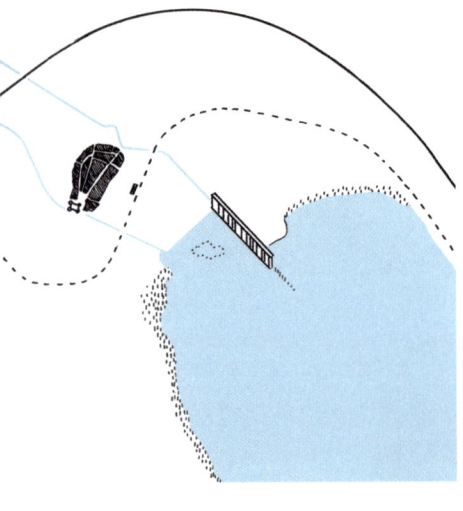

Rügen, Heinrich Tessenow, 1936

Am Anfang steht eine Idee von Pipilotti Rist für die Arteplage Yverdon: Heiraten für 24 Stunden. Ein Jahr vor Eröffnung der expo.02 wird die Idee von den Szenografen der Gruppe «aggregat» in eine greifbare Geschichte und Form umgesetzt, eine Sequenz aus sechs Räumen; der inhaltliche Ablauf kommt einem Ritual gleich. Als Standort ist der Militärsteg auf der Mole zwischen Thielle und Seebucht vorgesehen und die Architekten werden für eine Hülle um die sechs Räume angefragt.

Die für diesen aussergewöhnlichen Ort unzureichend gestellte Anfrage verführt dazu, einen Wald von 151 9 m hohen, unregelmässig gestellten und leuchtend farbigen Stützen mit einem 150 m langen und 6 m breiten Dach vorzuschlagen. Boden, Decke, Brüstung und die Lattenschürze im Wasser sind blendend weiss, ebenso der flankierende schlanke Pavillon. Auf drei Seiten ist er mit Stoff bekleidet, auf der Hafenseite mit Dachpappe. Dank einem grossen Fenster ergibt sich ein reicher Dialog zwischen innen und aussen. Das Ganze soll festlich-heiter sein. Der Stützenwald komplettiert das Ritual szenografisch um Hin- und Rückweg, durch wechselnde Dichten differenziert. Darüber hinaus aber wird ein öffentlicher Raum geschaffen, zugänglich für alle Besucher der Arteplage und offen für unterschiedliche Aneignungen, ein Ort ohne Ausstellung, der mit dem Dunst der Wolke («le Nuage») zum «barocken Setting» gerinnt.

Und nicht zuletzt leistet der Stützenwald das, was die offiziellen Expo-Ikonen erfolgreich tun: Er inszeniert Landschaft. Sie ist – blickt man auf den See – unspektakulär, nicht überreizt, aber von einer grosszügigen, von keinem Berg gebrochenen Weite, die sich oft, wenn die Grenze zwischen See und Himmel verschwimmt, ins Unendliche dehnt. Schiffe tauchen am Horizont auf oder verschwinden dort, der See wird zum Meer, und jenseits ahnt man einen anderen Kontinent. Die Wolken darüber erzählen von derselben Weite.

Pavillon Oui!, expo.02, Yverdon-les-Bains

It started with an idea by Pipilotti Rist for the Arteplage Yverdon: Getting married for 24 hours. A year before the expo.02 was opened, the idea was turned into a tangible story and form by scenographers of the "aggregat" group. It is a sequence of six rooms; the order of content is like a ritual. The location is the military runway on the jetty between the river Thielle and the bay, and the architects were contracted to produce a shell around the six rooms.

The inadequately tendered commission for this exceptional location enticed the architects to propose a forest of 151 nine-metre tall, irregularly positioned glowing coloured columns supporting a 150 m long and 6 m wide roof. The floor, ceiling, parapet and the lattice apron in the water are radiant white, as is the slim, flanking pavilion. Fabric covers three sides, while the harbour side is clad in roofing felt. A large window creates a rich dialogue between the inside and outside. The ensemble should have a light, festive character. The forest of columns becomes part of the scenography and completes the ritual providing a way there and a way back, and is varied with alternating densities. Moreover, a public space is created that is accessible for all visitors to the Arteplage and is open for a variety of uses, a place without exhibits that transforms into a "Baroque setting" in combination with the mist of the cloud ("le Nuage").

Last but not least, the forest of columns also achieves what the official Expo icons successfully manage, namely staging landscapes. Looking upon the lake, it is unspectacular and not over-imposing. However, its expansive breadth is uninterrupted by any mountain, thereby often allowing the lake and the sky to merge and stretch into the infinite distance.

Ships appear on the horizon, the lake becomes a sea and beyond it, one can sense another continent. The clouds above reflect the same expanse.

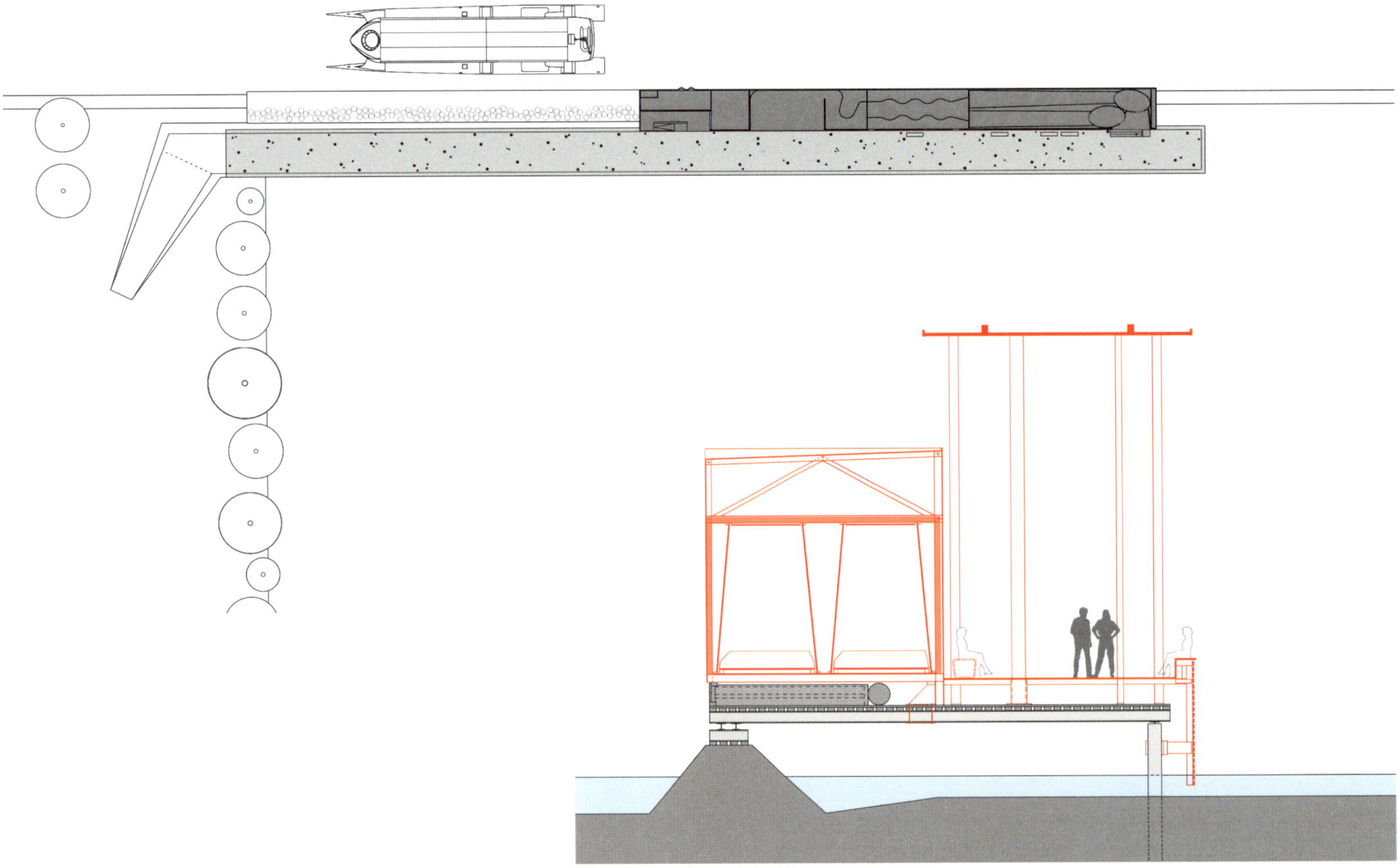

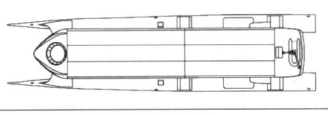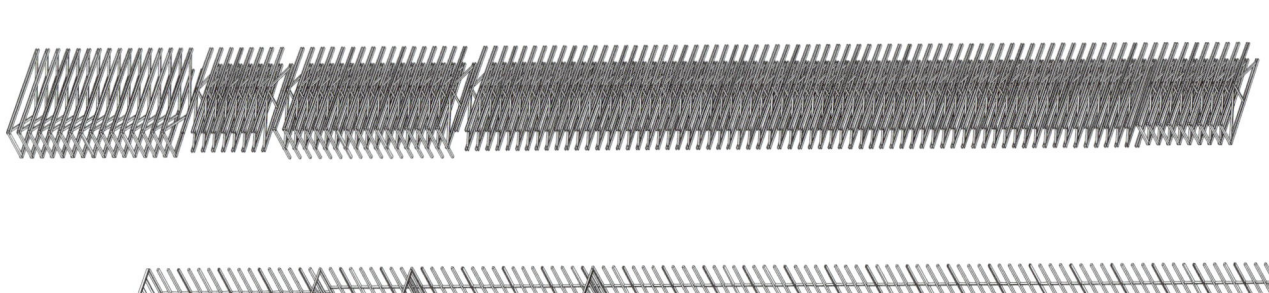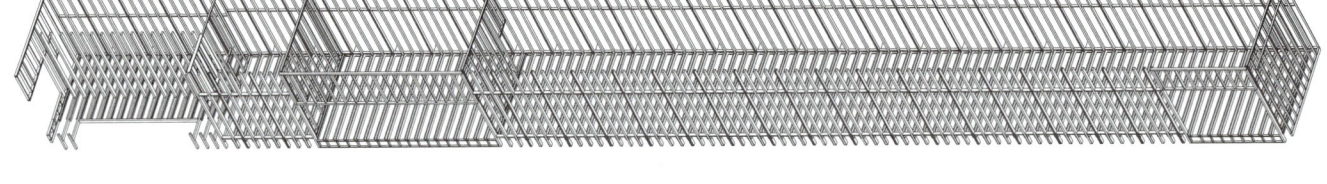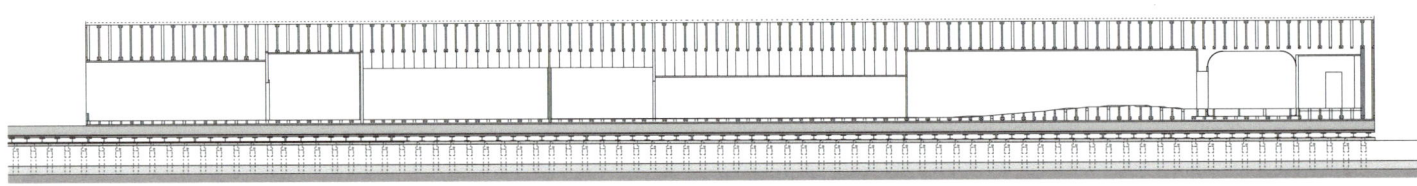

Umbau und Erweiterung Musikinsel Kloster Rheinau

Conversion and extension of the Rheinau Monastery

Wettbewerb / Competition: 2009
Bauingenieur / Civil engineer: Walt + Galmarini, Zürich
Aussenraumgestaltung / Landscape design: Rotzler Krebs Partner Winterthur
Auftraggeber / Client: Hochbauamt Kanton Zürich / Canton of Zurich Construction Authority

Die Anlage diente vom 8. Jahrhundert bis 1862 als Kloster und nach Abbrüchen, Um- und Neubauten vor allem im westlichen Bereich von 1867 bis 2000 als psychiatrische Klinik. Seither wird ein grosser Teil der Gebäude nicht mehr genutzt. Diese sollen mit neuen Programmen wieder belebt werden. Der Projektnachweis ist in unterschiedlichen Eingriffstiefen und Massstäben zu erbringen. Ein Gästezimmer für das vorgesehene Musikzentrum zeigt detailliert, wie die ehemaligen Mönchszellen räumlich, materiell sowie haustechnisch ertüchtigt werden sollen. Der Restaurationsbetrieb wird zum Anlass genommen, dem Innern des mehrfach veränderten Mühlesaalbaus eine seiner würdevollen Geschichte entsprechende neue Ordnung zu geben. Ein neuer Treppenkern, kombiniert mit einem Holz-Beton-Verbundträgerrost, ordnet die Grundrisse und Geschosse. Die Treppe erschliesst den wiederhergestellten Festsaal derart, dass dessen räumliche Kraft ungebrochen zur Wirkung kommt. Für die Hauswirtschafts- und Berufswahlschulen wird der sogenannte Wolffsbau aus dem 19. Jahrhundert im Inneren neu organisiert. Das Gebäude aus den 1970er-Jahren beim Eingang zum Hof wird durch einen Neubau ersetzt. Da sich programmatisch nicht begründen lässt, weshalb sich dieser im Ausdruck von den übrigen nicht sakralen Bauten unterscheiden sollte, ist er von derselben Schlichtheit. Wesentlich ist seine raumdefinierende Aufgabe. Weitere kleine Massnahmen schärfen die Unterscheidung räumlicher Charaktere wie *extra* und *intra muros*. Das fehlende Stück Klostermauer wird wieder aufgebaut. Den Hofzugang bildet anstelle eines schmiedeisernen Tores eine Ädikula – ein Faltwerk aus Metall.

The building complex served as a monastery between the 8th century and 1862. After successive demolition, conversion and new building measures, above all to the western section, it was used as a psychiatric clinic between 1867 and 2000. Since then, a large part of the building has remained unused. The intention is to revitalize it with new programmes. The project requires measures of various depths and scales. A guest room for the planned music centre shows in detail how the former monks' and patients' rooms are to be enhanced in terms of their space, materials and building technology. The restaurant business is used as an occasion to create a new, suitably respectable order for the interior of the Mühlesaalbau building, which had to undergo several conversions in the past. A new stairwell, combined with a wood-cement bonded girder construction orders the ground plans and floors. The stairs provide access to the restored festival hall in a way that enhances its uninterrupted spatial effect. The interior of the so-called Wolffsbau from the 19th century is reorganised for the home economics and vocational schools, while the 1970s building at the entrance is replaced by a new building. There are hardly any reasons why its expression should be different from the other non-religious buildings. It has the same simplicity and its spatially defining task is especially important. Further smaller measures enhance the distinction between the spatial characters, such as *extra* and *intra muros*. The missing section of the monastery wall is rebuilt. One enters the court by walking through a folded metal structure called an *aedicule*, rather than a wrought-iron gate.

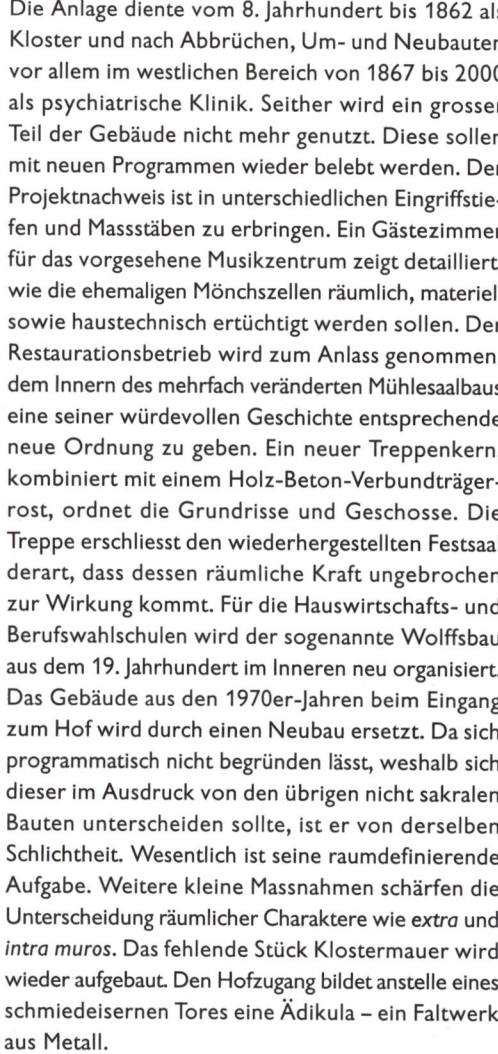

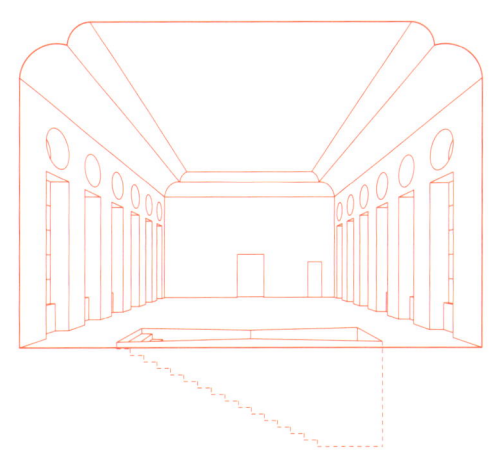
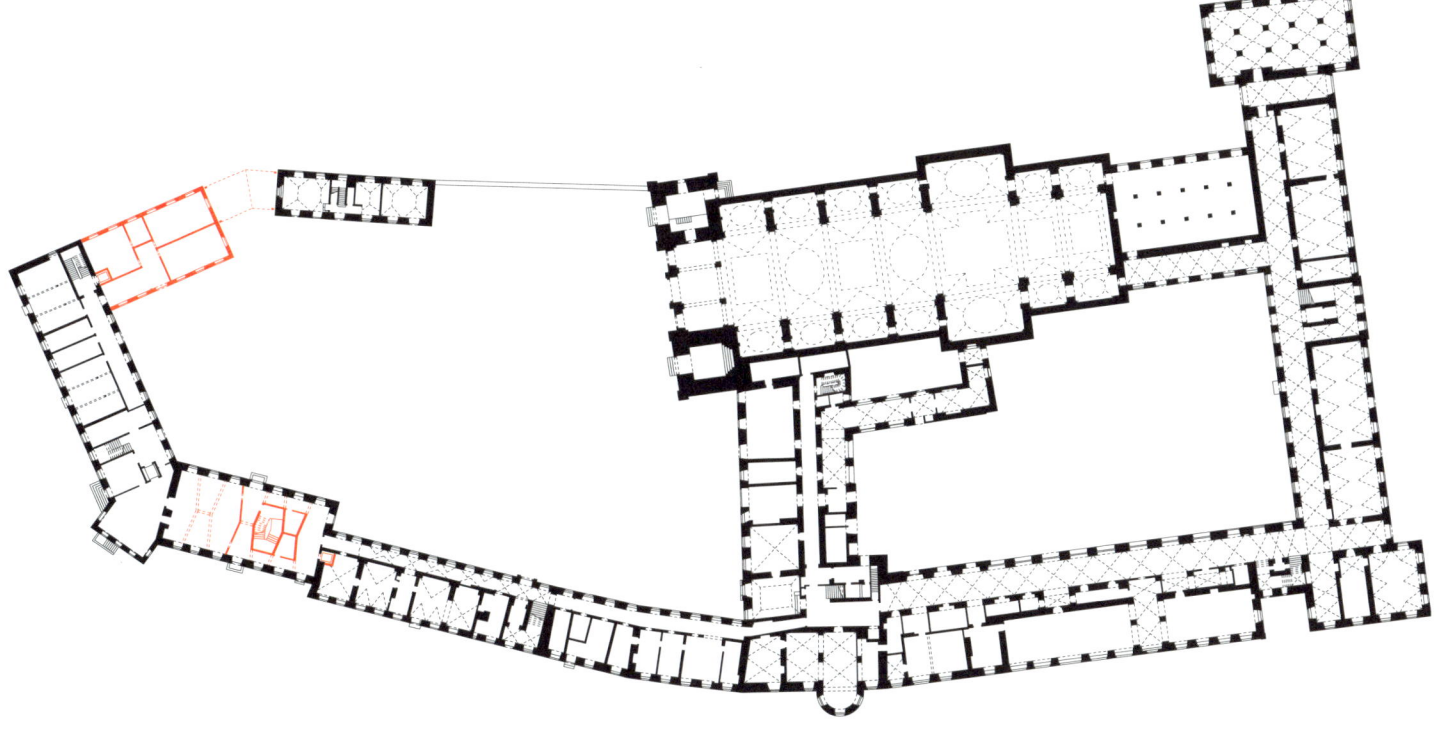
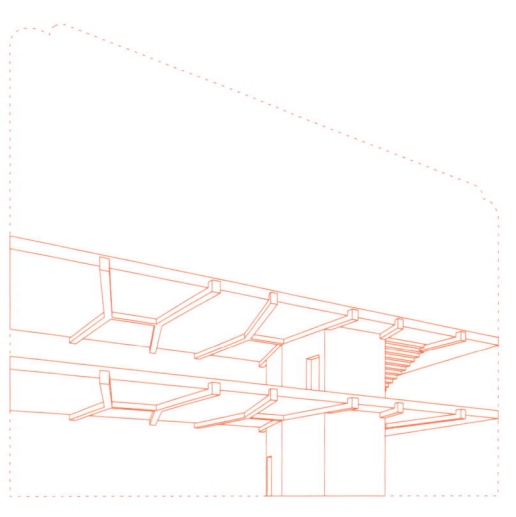

Areal Feldbach, Steckborn
Feldbach site, Steckborn

Wettbewerb / Competition: 1995
Auftraggeber / Client: Gemeinde Steckborn / City of Steckborn

Im Feldbachdelta westlich des Städtchens Steckborn am Bodensee stand im 13. Jahrhundert eine Burg, später ein Kloster. Nach 1848 wurde es gewerblich genutzt. In der Folge entwickelte sich das Gebiet zwischen See und Hauptstrasse zu einem ausgedehnten Industrieareal. In den 1970er-Jahren, nach der Abwanderung der Industrie, ging es in den Besitz der Gemeinde über. Mit Abbrüchen wurde Land für einen Park und für Parkplätze gewonnen. Heute werden die nach dem Brand von 1895 erhaltenen Teile des Klosters zusammen mit einem Neubau als Hotel genutzt. Die Bucht wurde zum Jachthafen ausgebaut. Ein Teil der Fabrikgebäude dient dem Gewerbe, ein anderer Freizeiteinrichtungen. Die Wettbewerbsaufgabe, der Bau von Schulräumen für die Oberstufe, wird über die Programmerfüllung hinaus genutzt, um die städtebauliche Situation zu klären. Die aufgebrochene Struktur, bestehend aus Industriehallen und einer Sport- und Mehrzweckhalle, wird um den ähnlich hohen Baukörper der Schule ergänzt. Das neue Ensemble bildet eine Raumfigur. In ihr kreuzen sich die wichtigsten Wege. Gleichzeitig wird auf der Südseite der Park erweitert. Im Westen wird zudem eine historische Häusergruppe arrondiert und verdichtet, östlich eine Reihe von gleichen Holzhäusern komplettiert und zum See hin werden die Zimmerflügel des Hotels erweitert. Die Eingriffe folgen der inneren Logik der jeweiligen Struktur.

In the 13th century, a castle was built on the Feldbach delta to the west of the small town of Steckborn. It later became a monastery. After 1848, it was used for industrial purposes. Over the years, the area between the lake and the main street developed into an extensive industrial estate. In the 1970s, following industrial decline, it became the propriety of the council and buildings were demolished to create new land for a park and parking space. Today, the parts of the monastery that survived the 1895 fire are used together with a new building as a hotel. The bay has been extended to create a yacht marina. Some of the factory buildings are still used for business, while others accommodate leisure activities. To clarify the urban planning situation, the project goes beyond fulfilling the competition task of building classrooms for a secondary school. The remaining structure of industrial halls, a sports hall and a multifunctional hall is complemented by the similarly tall school building. The new ensemble forms a spatial figure, with most passages crossing inside it. At the same time, the park on the south side is extended. To the west, a historical group of houses is also rounded off and densified, to the east a row of identical wooden buildings is completed, while towards the lake, the hotel's wings accommodating the rooms are extended. The measures follow the inner logic of the given structure.

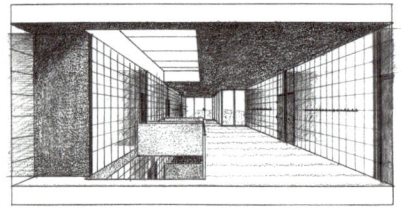

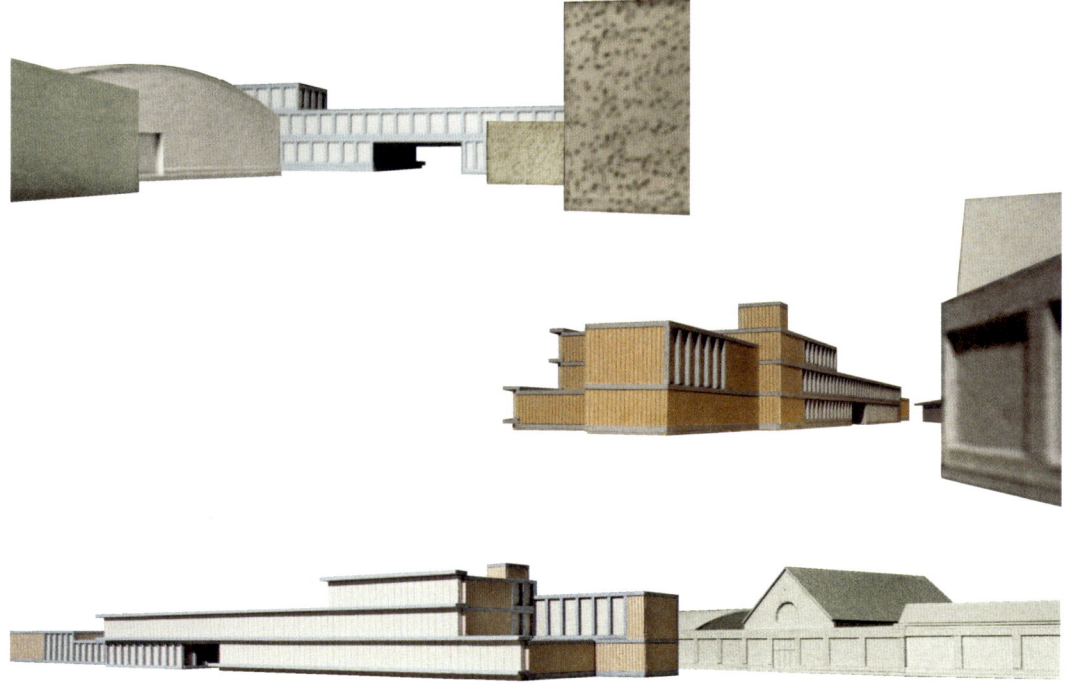

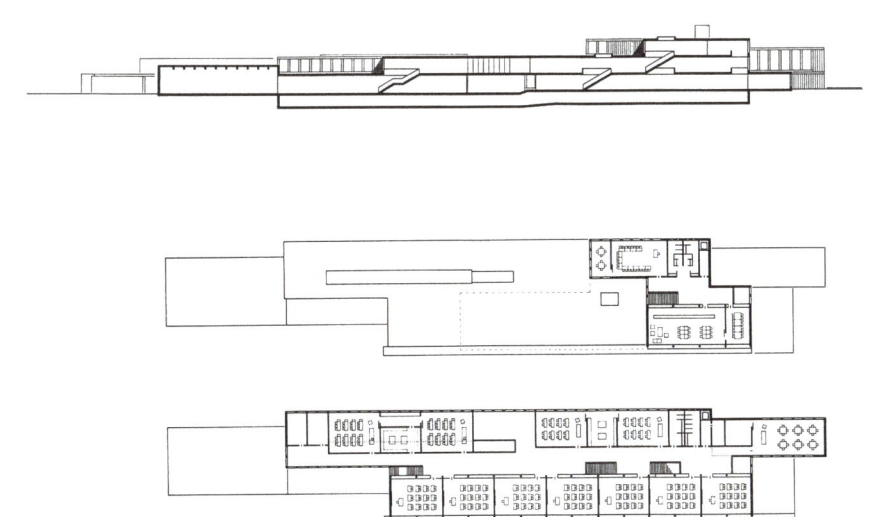
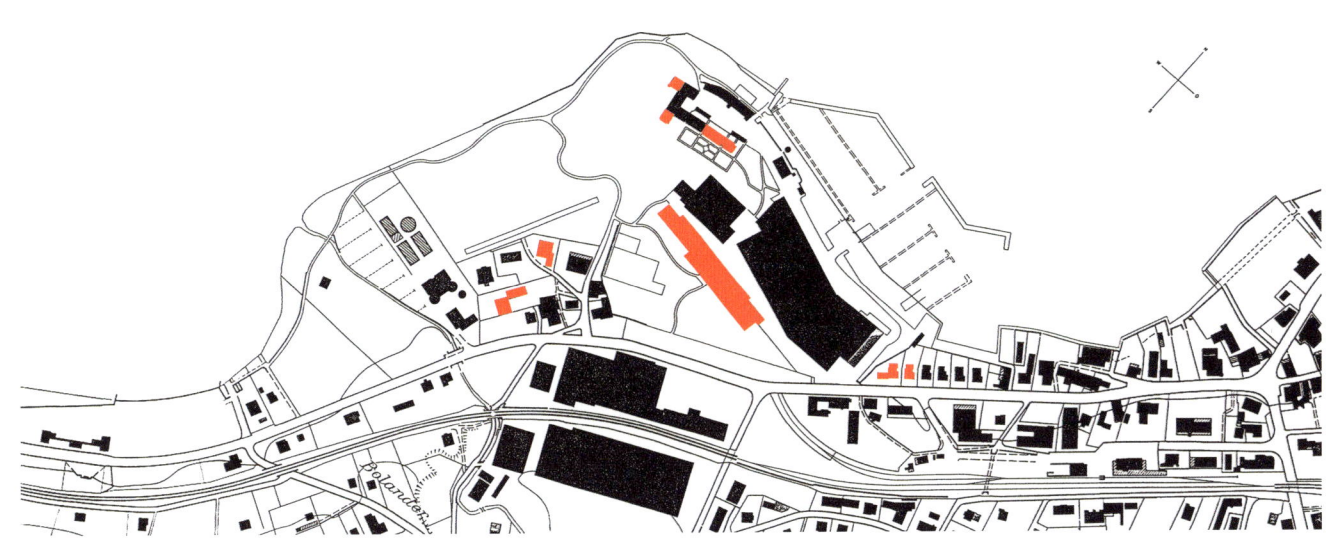
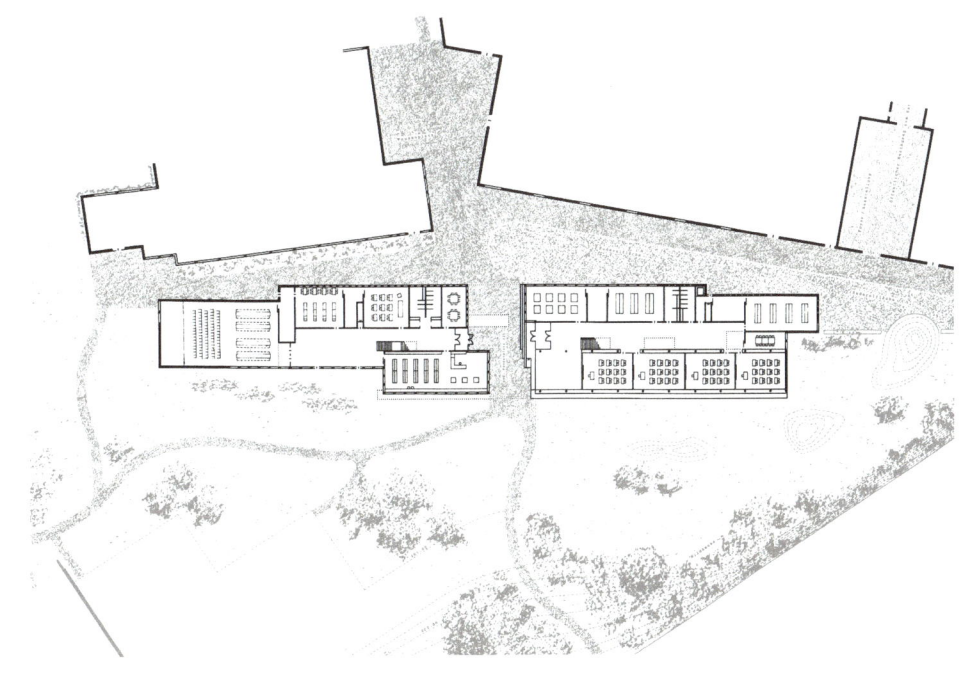

Maag-Areal Plus, Zürich

Maag Areal Plus, Zurich

Studienauftrag / Study contract: 2000
mit / with: Diener & Diener
Architekten, Basel
Masterplan / Master plan: 2004
Aussenraumgestaltung / Landscape
design: Rotzler Krebs Partner,
Winterthur
Auftraggeber / Client: Maag Holding,
Coop, Welti Furrer, Stadt Zürich

Im Anhang zu den Sonderbauvorschriften für das Gebiet Maag-Areal Plus, 2003, steht zu lesen: «1. Bebauungskonzept. Die Strukturen, die auf dem Areal vorhanden sind, werden der künftigen Entwicklung zugrunde gelegt. Dabei geht es weniger um bestehende Gebäude oder Anlagen als vielmehr um Regeln, die diesem Areal teilweise offensichtlich, teilweise versteckt eingeschrieben sind. Sie betreffen den künftigen Umgang mit diesem Ort über die Zeit. Vier unterschiedliche Bereiche machen das ganze Planungsgebiet Maag-Areal Plus aus: das eigentliche Maag-Areal, der Maaghof, der Bereich angrenzend an die Familiengärten, die Grundstücke entlang der Pfingstweidstrasse. Bezüglich Freiraum und Bebauungsmuster haben die vier Bereiche ihre jeweils spezifischen Merkmale und Regeln. Diese unterstützen auf jeweils unterschiedliche Art: a) die Verzahnung der Stadträume an den Rändern des Areals, b) die ruhige Mitte, c) die Durchlässigkeit der Erdgeschossebene, d) die Entstehung eines fliessenden Freiraumkontinuums in der Form eines durchgehenden Stadtbodens, e) das Weiterentwickeln von spannungsvollen Raumabfolgen mit vielfältigen Sichtbezügen. Für alle Bereiche sieht das Bebauungskonzept klar geschnittene Baukörper vor. Im öffentlichen Bereich soll eine ruhige Raumwirkung erzielt werden. [...] Im Dachbereich ist eine ruhige und klare Silhouette anzustreben. [...] Eine Markierung der Ecken oder eine durchgehende Verstärkung der Arealränder durch höhere Gebäude ist nicht erwünscht.» Intendiert ist eine zeitgenössische Interpretation der Industrietypologie. Nebenstehende Pläne und das Modell stellen eine Möglichkeit der allmählichen Umsetzung des Bebauungskonzeptes dar, in dem auch Umbauten ihren Platz haben sollen.

The appendix to the special building regulations for the 2003 Maag Areal Plus area states: "1st development concept. The structures that exist on the estate form the basis of the future development. More than existing buildings or facilities, these structures, which are partially explicit and partially hidden, are the rules inscribed in the site. They affect the future handling of the location. Four different areas define the entire Maag Areal Plus estate: the actual Maag-Areal, the Maaghof, the area adjoining the family gardens, and the properties along Pfingstweidstrasse. With respect to the development pattern, the four areas each have their own characteristics and rules. They are supported in different ways by: a) the interlocking urban spaces at the edge of the estate, b) the calm centre, c) the permeability of the ground floor level, d) the creation of a fluent continuum of open space in the form of a continuous urban floor level, e) the further development of exciting spatial sequences with diverse visual references. The development concept plans clearly defined building volumes for all areas. A calm spatial effect is intended for the public area. [...] In the roof area, a peaceful, clear silhouette is required. [...] A marking of the corners and a continuous reinforcement of the estate's periphery through taller buildings are not desired." The aim was to achieve a contemporary interpretation of the industrial typology. Accompanying plans and a model present the option of gradually implementing the development concept, which should also include conversion measures.

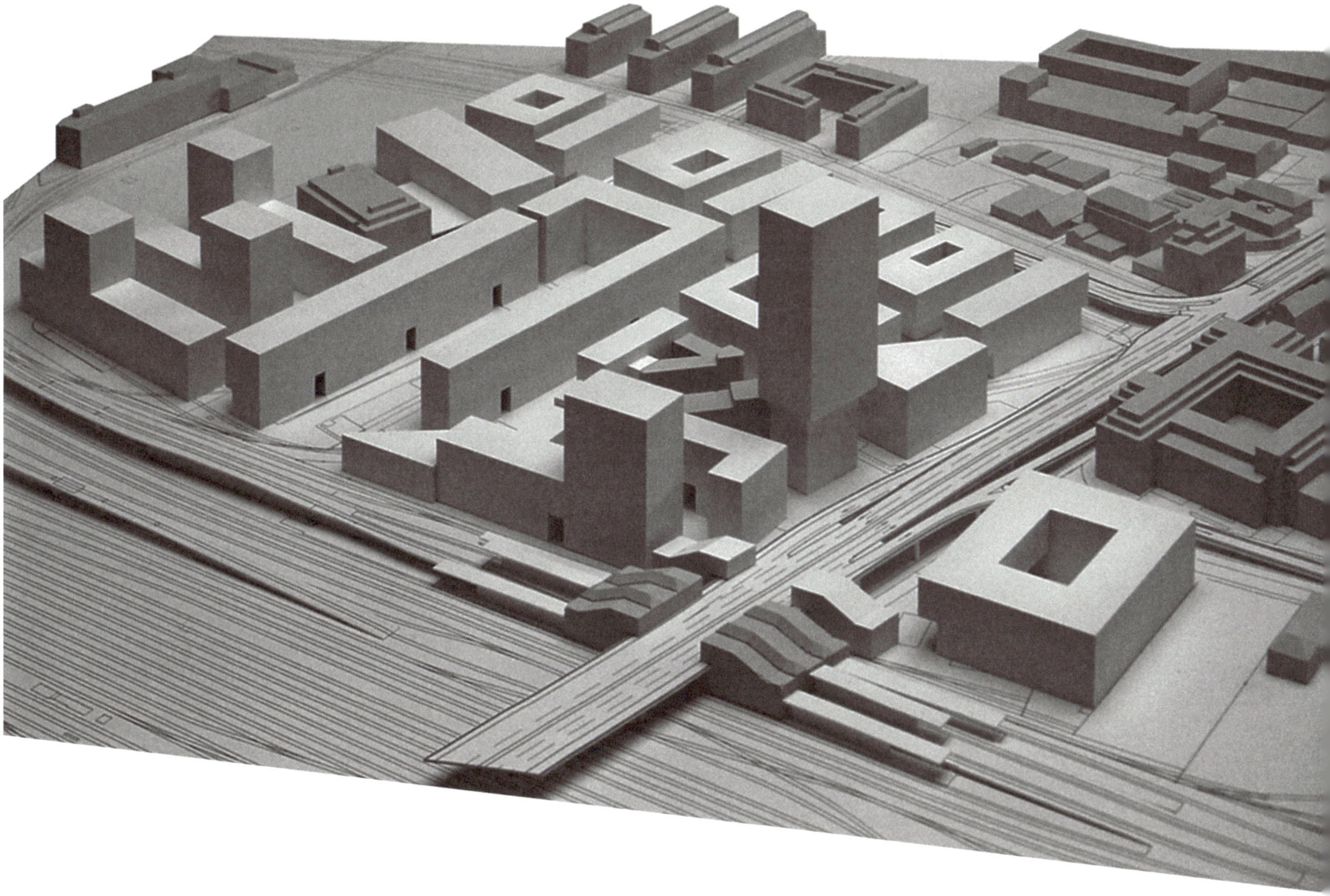

Städtebauliche Studie Lagerplatz (Sulzerareal), Winterthur

Urban development study, Lagerplatz (Sulzerareal), Winterthur

Studienauftrag / Study contract: 2006
Masterplan / Master plan: 2007
Aussenraumgestaltung / Landscape design: Jane Sörensen, Hamburg; Günter Vogt, Zürich
Auftraggeber / Client: Sulzer Immobilien, Die Post, Stadt Winterthur

Ziel ist eine städtebauliche Ordnung und die Definition der zugehörigen Regeln als Grundlage für die anschliessende Übersetzung in Rechtsinstrumente. Seit Jahren ist dieser Teil der ehemals «verbotenen Stadt» offen, zwischengenutzt und vital und die Annäherung von Grundeigentümern und staatlichen Stellen weit fortgeschritten.

Zur Studie: Ausgangspunkt gegenüber neuen Bedürfnissen ist der Bestand und die genaue Kenntnis seiner materiellen und immateriellen Werte. Eine schrittweise Transformation soll möglich sein ohne vorgeschriebene Abfolge. Tabula rasa ist keine Option. Tendenzen werden deutlicher gemacht: Die schmalen Gebäude längs der Strasse werden verlängert und somit wird der Zwischenraum, die Gasse, ausgeprägter; eine starke Figur mit eigener Identität entsteht. Gegenüber, längs den Geleisen, werden Hofgebäude mit unterschiedlichen Tiefen vorgeschlagen (gemäss dem Prinzip der «Footprints» der Industriehallen): ein Wohnhaus mit Gartenhof, ein Gebäude für Büros oder eine Schule. Zwischen den beiden der «Square» und das Gebäude genannte «Joker» für Büros, Wohnungen, ein Hotel oder auch ein Museum. Die beiden Ordnungen generieren die hierarchische Figur des öffentlichen Raumes – das «Rückgrat» –, sie strukturiert das Areal. Ihre gestische Form lädt ein zum Eintreten und führt auch wieder hinaus. Diese Raumfigur wiederum gliedern Pavillons. Ihre Nutzung ist öffentlich. Die Zeichnung des «Square» (heute ist er ein Lagerplatz) wird präzisiert und verbindet die Längsachse mit dem Gleisfeld. Die Durchlässigkeit im Erdgeschoss und Sichtbezüge schaffen räumliche Tiefen und Beziehungen und erleichtern die Orientierung.

Der Vorschlag der Studie, die auch als Umnutzung viel beachtete Architekturschule in der angestammten Halle 180 zu belassen («Never change a winning horse») oder sogar zu erweitern, wird mit einer Machbarkeitsstudie vertieft.

The aim is to set the principles of urban development and to define appropriate rules as the basis for subsequent translation into legal instruments. For years, this part of the formerly "forbidden city" has been open, used on an interim basis and lively, while approaches between owners and city authorities were well advanced.

As to the study, the starting point regarding new requirements is the existing structure and a precise knowledge of its material and immaterial values. Gradual transformation should be possible, without a mandatory sequence. A tabula rasa is not an option.

Tendencies are made clearer: the slim buildings along the street will be lengthened, making the interspace, the alley, more distinctive, to create a strong figure with its own identity. Opposite, along the railway tracks, a courtyard building with differing depths is proposed (according to the principle of the "footprints" of the industrial buildings): a residential building with a garden courtyard, a building for offices or a school. Between the two buildings lies the "square" and the building known as "the joker", for offices, apartments, a hotel or a museum. The two orders generate the hierarchical figure of the public space – the "backbone" – structuring the estate. Its gesturing form invites people to enter and leads out of the area. Pavilions structure this spatial figure. Their use is public. The design of the "square" (where a storage yard is located today) is specified and connects the longitudinal axis to the area of the train tracks. The permeability of the ground floor and the visual relationships create spatial depth and interconnections, while also facilitating orientation.

The study's proposal to keep and even extend the architectural school in the established Hall 180, which is itself a widely admired conversion, will be further investigated in a feasibility study.

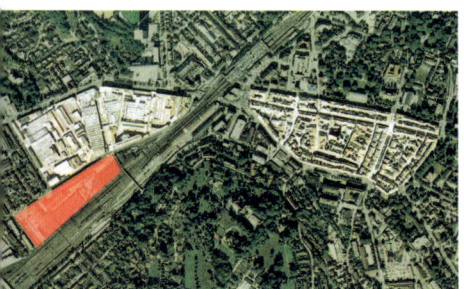

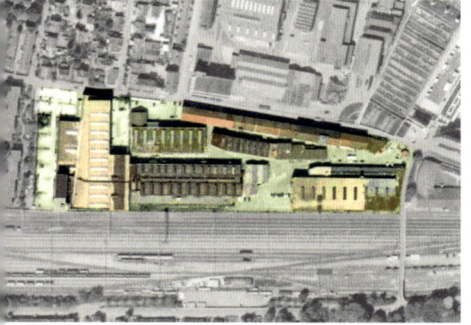

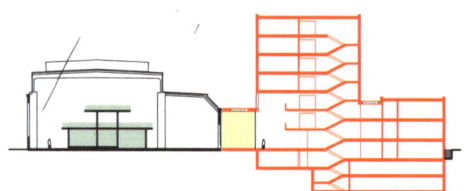

FORUM
PFORTE
GARTENHOF
SQUARE
G L E I S R A U M G L E I S R A U M

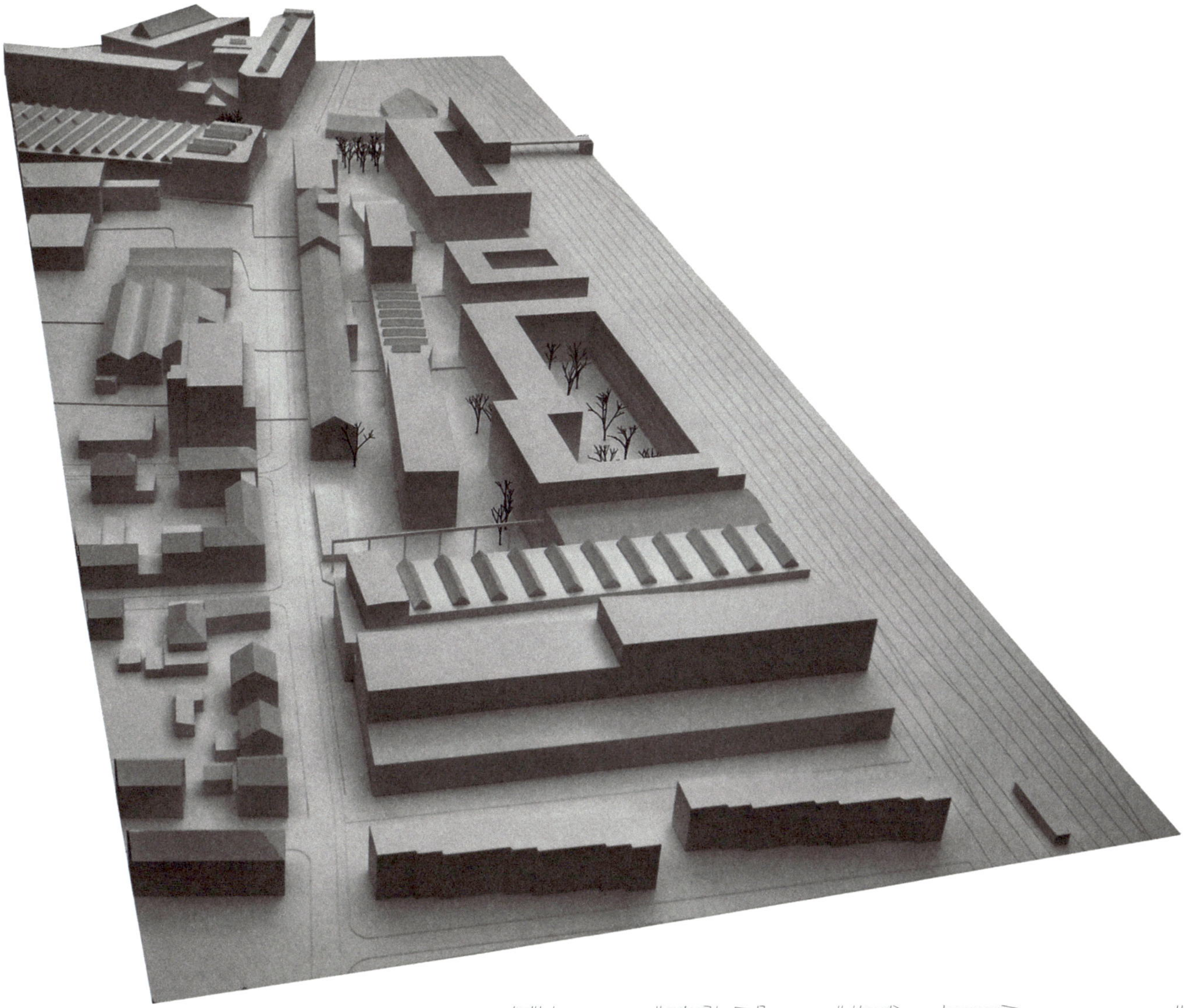

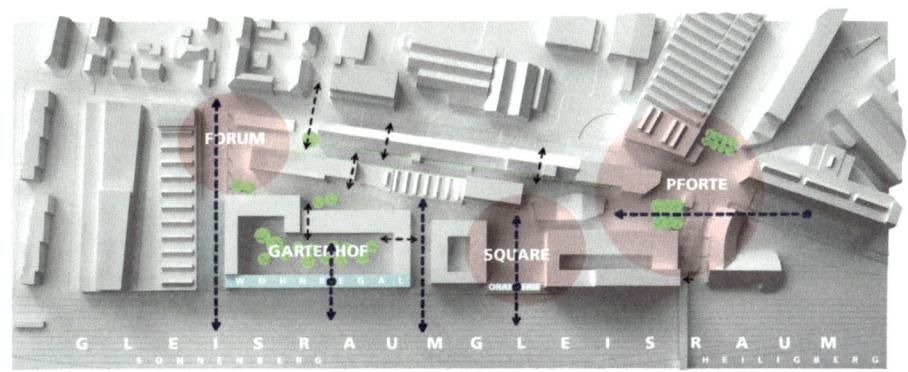

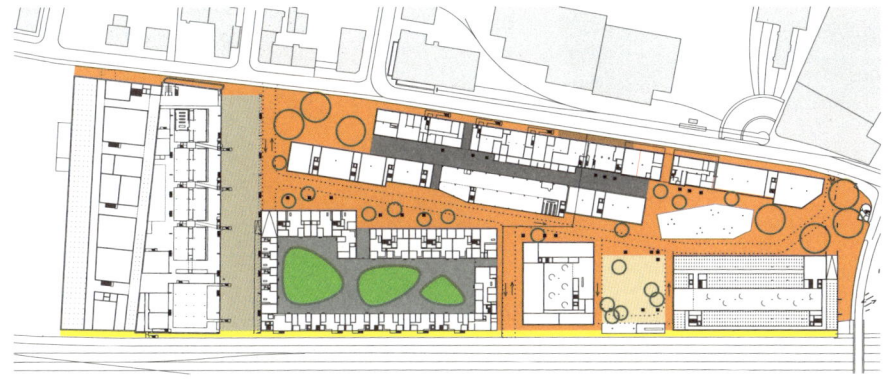

Städtebauliche Studie Tour Henri, Fribourg

Urban planning study, Tour Henri, Fribourg

Studienauftrag / Study contract: 2011–2012
Aussenraumgestaltung / Landscape design: Hager Landschaftsarchitekten, Zürich
Auftraggeber / Client: Stadt Fribourg, Universität / City of Fribourg, University

Merianplan 1642: Die Strassenachsen mit Stadttoren in Richtung Romont/Lausanne bzw. Avenches/Payerne lassen abseits der städtischen Aktivitäten und Bebauungen sozusagen eine «stille Ecke» entstehen. Die Tour Henri markiert den Eckpunkt.
Dufourkarte 1860: Unabhängig vom Verlauf der mittelalterlichen Stadtbefestigung wird das Trassee der Bahnlinie Bern–Lausanne ins Gelände eingeschnitten. Die Zäsur in Form der Stadtmauer wird von der Zäsur Bahntrassee abgelöst. Sie wirkt bis heute. Die «stille Ecke» besteht weiterhin.
2011: Markante Bauten besetzen strategische Positionen: das Hôpital des Bourgeois, das Hochhaus mit seinem Sockelgebäude, die Universität von Honegger Dumas (1941) sowie eine Gruppe von Altbauten auf der westlichen Seite. Hier stehen etwas verloren die Tour Henri und ein Mauerrest. Die Geleise sind teils überbaut (Mensa), was die räumliche Trennung verstärkt. Die nicht bebauten Stellen sind eher unbestimmter Natur: Parkplätze, etwas Grün, ein paar Wege.
Studie 2011/12: Die heutige Mensa aus den 1980er-Jahren soll abgebrochen werden, um damit die Kraft des Universitätsgebäudes von 1941 – eine eigentliche «Stadtkrone» – für den Ort wiederzugewinnen. Die hauptsächlich von der Universität geforderten neuen grossen Volumina stabilisieren den Zwischenraum. Die «stille Ecke» wird zu einem Park mit neuen Wegen und bereinigten Sichtverbindungen. Der geklärte Raum wird nie konfliktfrei sein. Die Verletzung durch das Bahntrassee ist wortwörtlich zu einschneidend – einem Schmiss gleich, welcher das Gesicht des Mitglieds einer schlagenden Verbindung für den Rest seines Lebens verunstaltet.

Merian plan, 1642: The thoroughfare axes with city gates towards Romont/Lausanne and Avenches/Payerne have created a "quiet corner" outside the urban activities and developments. The Tour Henri marks its corner.
Dufour map, 1860: The Bern-Lausanne railway line is cut into the terrain independently of the course of the medieval city fortifications. The caesura of the city walls is replaced by the caesura of the railway track. The effect still exists today. The "quiet corner" remains.
2011: Striking buildings occupy strategic positions: the Hôpital des Bourgeois, the high-rise building with a base, the university by Honegger Dumas (1941) and a group of old buildings on the western side. The Tour Henri and a remnant of the wall stand there rather forlornly. The railway lines are partially covered with building structures (students' canteen), thus enhancing the spatial separation. The undeveloped areas are rather non-descript: a park field, a green area and a few paths.
Study 2011/12: Today's canteen from the 1980s is to be demolished to regain the power of the 1941 university dominating the city – like a "Stadtkrone". The large volumes mainly required by the university stabilize the intermediary space. The "quiet corner" becomes a park with a new system of pathways and clearer visual relationships. The clarified space will never be free of conflicts. The wound created by the railway line is literally too incisive – like a scar that marks the face of a student fraternity member for the rest of his life.

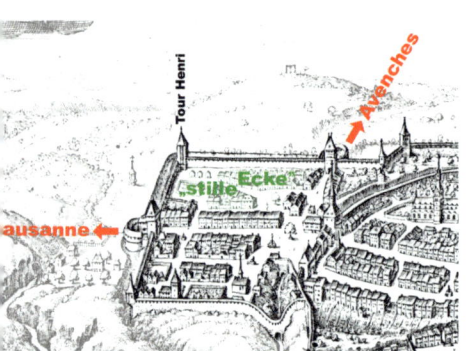

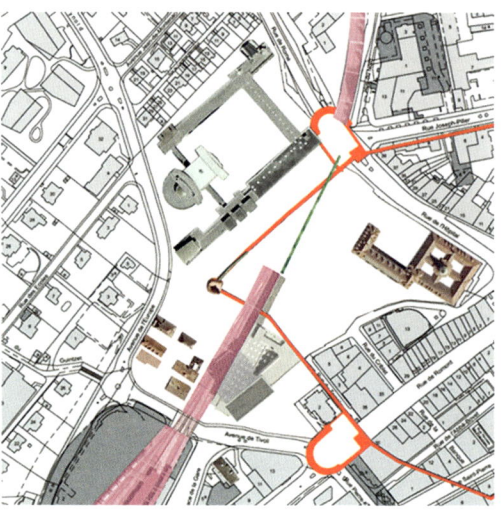

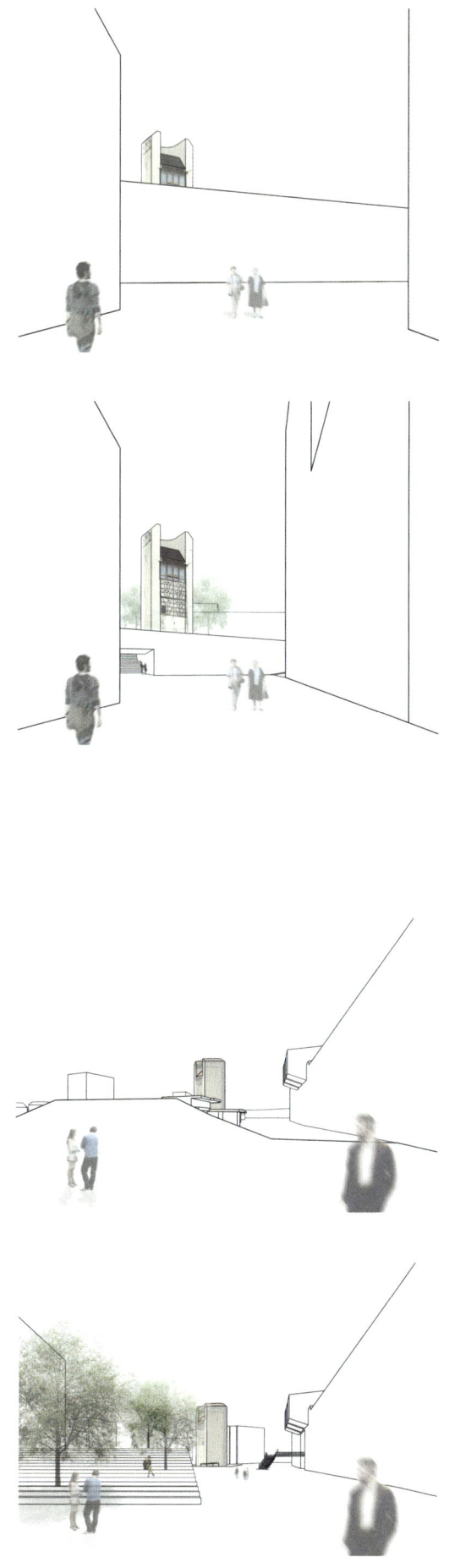

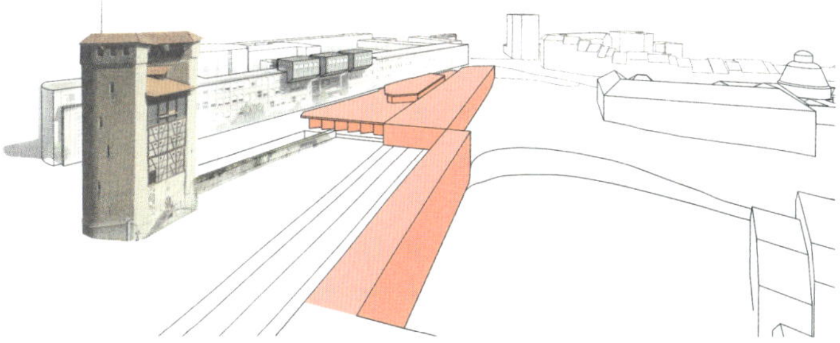

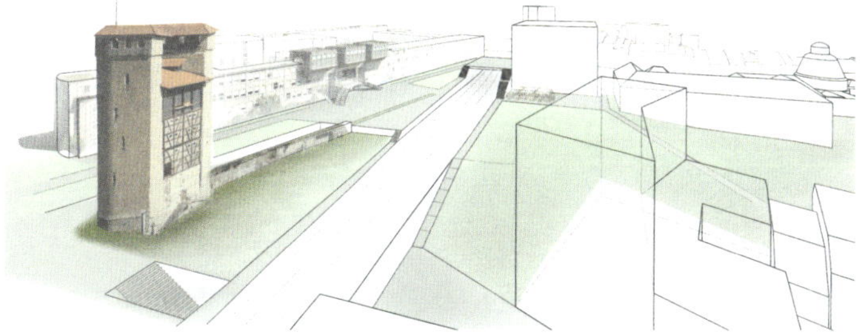

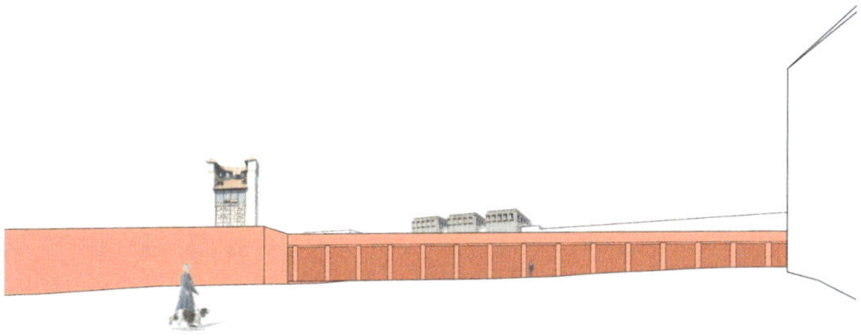

67

Um- und Anbau Villa Rainhof, Zürich

Conversion and extension, Villa Rainhof, Zurich

Baujahr / Year of construction: 1867
Planerwahl / Competition: 2005
Planung und Ausführung / Planning and construction measure: 2005– 2008
Bauingenieur / Civil engineer: ATP Ingenieure, Zürich
Kunst /Artwork: Mbah Moses Godlove, Kamerun, Mirca Maffi, Zürich, Boesch Architekten, Bettina Köhler (Korreferat), Zürich
Auftraggeber / Client: Hochbauamt des Kantons Zürich / Canton of Zurich Construction Authority

Die Villa wurde auf einem Sattel des sanften Moränenhügels am damaligen Stadtrand von Zürich erbaut: mit drei repräsentativen Neurenaissancefassaden seeseitig und einer bedeutungslosen Rückseite zum bewaldeten Zürichberg hin. Der Eingang lag seitlich. In den 40er-Jahren wurde die Villa in ein Zweifamilienhaus umgebaut, was die Verlegung des Zugangs auf die Rückseite, Anpassungen des Grundrisses und eine neue Treppe erforderte. Im Innern wurde der gesamte Schmuck des 19. Jahrhunderts abgetragen. Ab den 80er-Jahren nutzte die ETH Zürich die Räume.

Mit dem jetzigen Umbau für die die Institute für Systematische Botanik und Pflanzenbiologie der Universität Zürich wird der Wandel zum Schulgebäude definitiv vollzogen. Der Grundriss wird geklärt, und mit einem Anbau erhält das Haus einen angemessenen Eingang, darüber das «Baumzimmer»: Das Haus wird endlich, seiner Lage entsprechend, zweigesichtig. Die Sanierung von Altlasten und die enorme technische Aufrüstung sind der unsichtbare Teil des Projektes. Die kahlen, nackten Räume warfen Fragen auf, welche mit einem neuen «Schmuckprogramm» beantwortet werden. Zarte Farbigkeit der Räume in den Hauptgeschossen, Gravuren im neuen Täfer, Schablonenmalerei an den Decken der Hallen und des Baumzimmers sowie sorgfältige Schreinerarbeiten geben den Räumen die nötige architektonische Dichte zurück. Die Wahl pflanzlicher Motive ist naheliegend. Zu simpel und unverbindlich wäre das Stilmittel Reduktion auch für den Anbau. Differenzierung der Gläser, Schmuckknöpfe im Obergeschoss und Gussreliefs auf den Pfeilern auf Augenhöhe, gerichtet wie die Koren am Erechtheion, das Fugenbild, der Farbton und die Textur des Betons ähnlich den auch aus Teilen zusammengesetzten und profilierten Sandsteinarbeiten am Haus, geben Mass und Verbindlichkeit.

The villa was built on the ridge of the gentle moraine hill on what was then the edge of the City of Zurich, with three representative façades on the lake side and an insignificant rear side facing the forested Zurichberg. The entrance was situated at the side. In the 1940s, the villa was converted into a two-family home, which required moving the entrance to the rear side, adapting the floor plan and the staircase. In the interior, the entire 19th century decoration was removed. The ETH Zurich has used the rooms from the 1980s onwards.

Its transformation into an educational building is definitively complete with the current conversion for the Institutes for Systematic Botany and Plant Biology at the University of Zurich. The floor plan is clearer and the building's extension gives it an appropriate entrance, above which is the "tree hall": the building finally has two faces, as is appropriate for its location. The project's invisible aspect was the removal of inherited waste and an enormous amount of technical upgrading. The bare, raw rooms raised questions that were answered with the new "decorative programme". Delicate colours for the rooms on the main floors, engravings on new panelling, stencil paintings on the ceilings of the hall and the "tree hall", as well as careful carpentry work restore the rooms' necessary architectural density. The choice of plant motifs is self-evident. The stylistic method of reduction would have been too simple and non-committal even for the extension. The distinguishing glasses, decorative buttons on the upper storey and the cast relief on the columns at eye-level, which are directed like the caryatids at the Erechtheum, the alignment of joints, the colour tone and the texture of the concrete similar to the sandstone work on the main building, which also consists of separately compiled and profiled sections, all provide scale, measure and commitment.

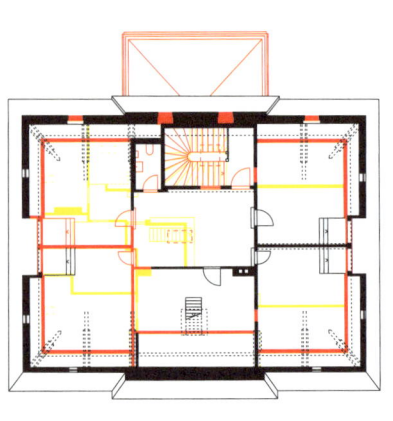

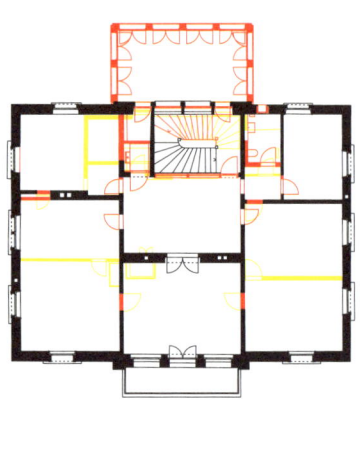

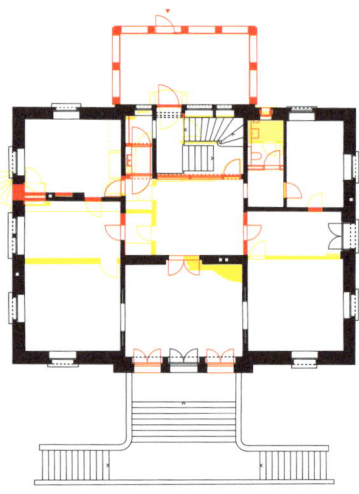

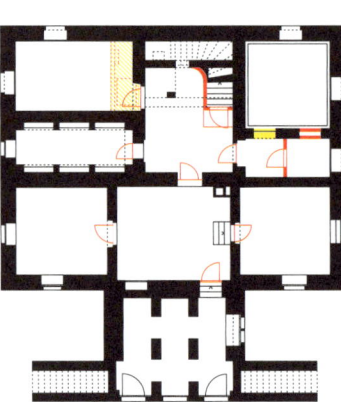

← Zürichsee　　　　　　　　　　　　　　　　　　　　　Zürichberg →

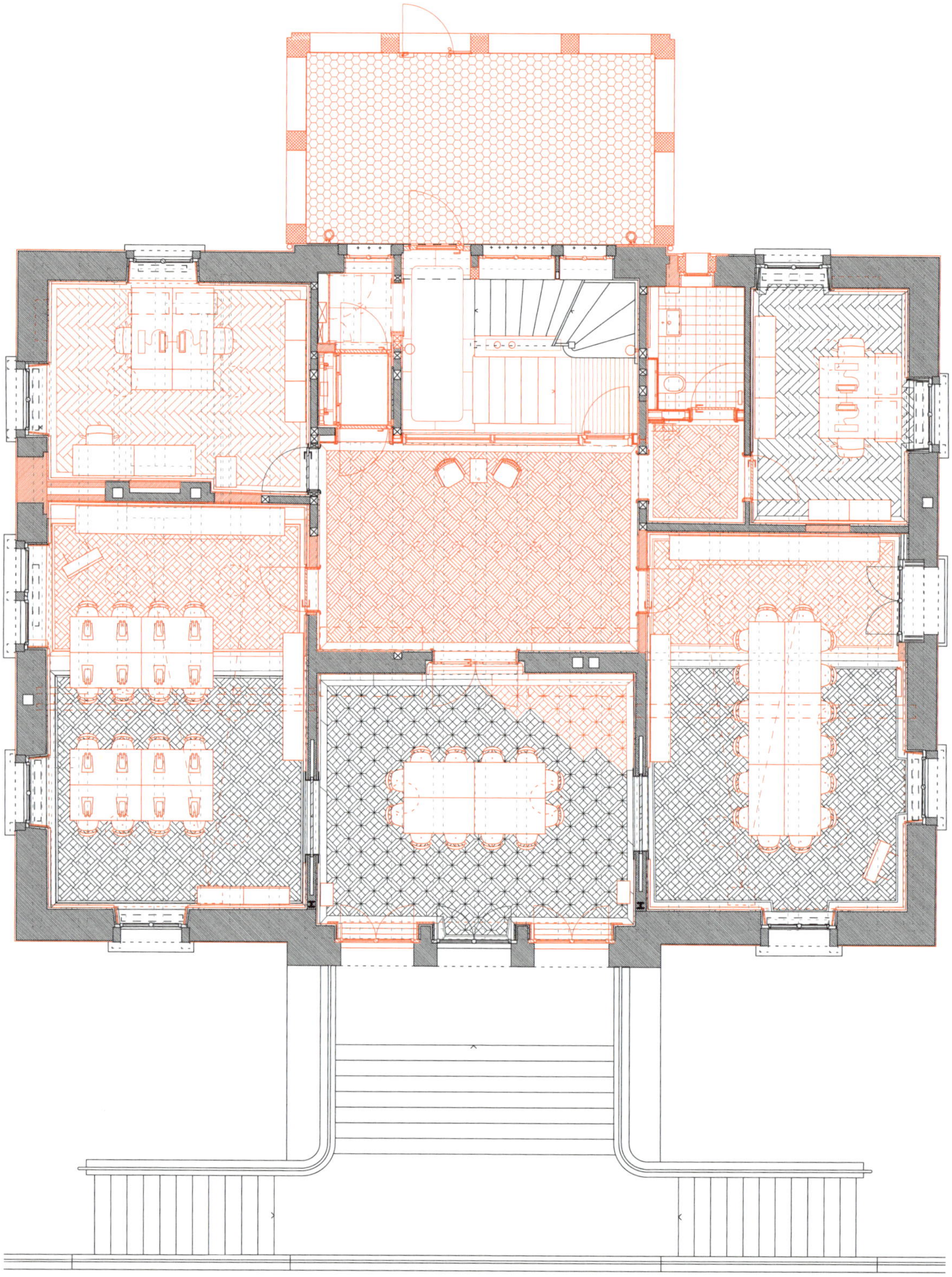

Instandsetzung, Umbau und Erweiterung, Kurtheater, Baden

Renovation, conversion and extension, Kurtheater, Baden

Baujahr / Year of construction: 1952
Architekten / Architects: Lisbeth Sachs/Otto Dorer Architekten, Baden
Studienauftrag / Study contract: 2007
Planung und Ausführung / Planning and construction measure: 2008–2020
Bauingenieur / Civil engineer: Walt + Galmarini, Zürich
Bauphysik / Structural physics: BWS, Winterthur
Auftraggeber / Client: Theaterstiftung der Region Baden/Wettingen

Zu Recht wird auf die Einzigartigkeit des Sachsfoyers verwiesen. Erst die ebenso grossartige Bewegungsführung von der Strasse zum Eingang durch die Halle über die Treppe zum Sachsfoyer und weiter in den Theaterraum bringt es zur Wirkung. Beides hat das Erweiterungsprojekt zu reflektieren. Seit 1955 wurden Erweiterungen vorgenommen, um das als Sommertheater gebaute Haus dem Ganzjahresbetrieb anzupassen. Damit und mit zusätzlichen Raumbedürfnissen (ca. 50 % mehr Fläche) läuft der Bau Gefahr, sein ursprünglich fein austariertes Gleichgewicht zu verlieren.

Das Projekt nimmt die einzigartige Weg-/Raumfigur ernst, indem es sich über die Vorgabe der Denkmalpflege, das Sachs-Foyer dürfe nicht tangiert werden, hinwegsetzt. Stattdessen wird die in diesem lichten Raum und seinen Treppenverbindungen angelegte Idee einer inneren Landschaft aufgenommen und weitergespielt. Einer Preziosen gleich wird das Foyer neu gefasst, liebevoll umfasst und zu einem einzigen statt der zwei geforderten Foyers entfaltet. Das alte gibt den Ton an für das Weiterbauen: räumlich, materiell und atmosphärisch.

Dem Wachsen des Foyers steht das Wachsen des eigentlichen Theaterbaus gegenüber. Das heute in mehreren Haupt- und Nebenbauten zergliederte Raumprogramm wird neu in einem kompakten Baukörper zusammengefasst. Bei allem Grösserwerden wird das alte Gleichgewicht in ein neues übergeführt. Das Bild bleibt vertraut. Zugleich gewinnt es – dem Ort und seiner Bedeutung angemessen – städtebaulich Gewicht und Präsenz.

Neu nimmt das Zyklopenauge des zuoberst im erweiterten Bühnenturm angelegten Proberaumes die Beziehung zur Landschaft jenseits der Limmat auf.

Das Preisgericht erkannte die Bedeutung und den Gewinn des produktiven Ungehorsams.

The unique nature of the Sachsfoyer has rightly been noted. Only the equally impressive guidance of the public from the street to the entrance through the hall, up the stairs to the Sachsfoyer and on into the auditorium creates the effect. The extension project had to reflect both of these aspects. Since 1955, extensions have been carried out to adapt the building, which was originally built as a summer theatre, for all-year use. As a result of this and the increased spatial requirements (around 50% more room), the building is in danger of losing its original finely balanced nature.

The project takes the unique spatial figure of paths and rooms seriously by ignoring the monument preservation office's requirement that the Sachsfoyer must not be affected. Instead, the idea of an inner landscape, already inherent in this light space with its stairway connections, is picked up on and reflected further. Like a gem, the foyer is newly contained, lovingly enveloped and unfolded to create a single hall, rather than the two requested foyers. The existing structure leads the way for the extension, in a spatial, atmospheric and material issues.

The foyer's expansion is faced by the growth of the theatre itself. Today's programme of rooms, including several main and auxiliary buildings, is newly pooled into one compact structure. Despite the great expansion, the building moves from one balanced form to a new one. The image remains familiar. At the same time, it maintains its urban significance and presence, as is appropriate for such a place and its importance.

The cyclops eye in the rehearsal room situated at the top of the extended stage tower creates a relationship with the landscape beyond the River Limmat.

The prize jury recognised the significance and advantages of such productive disobedience.

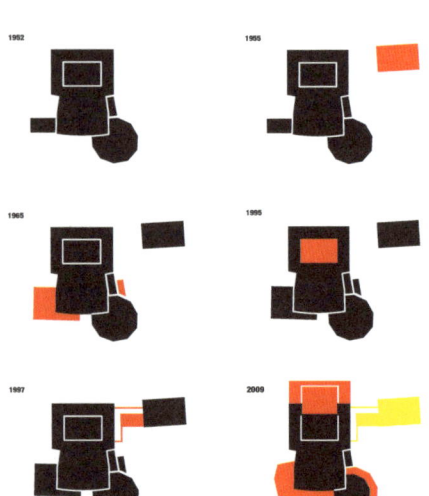

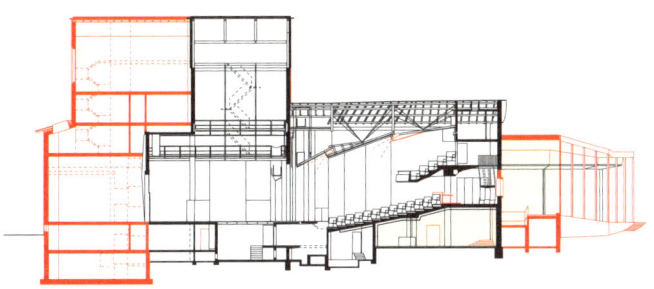
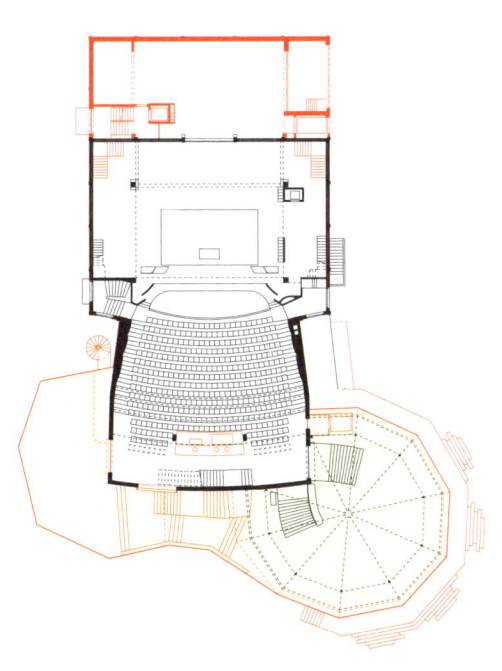

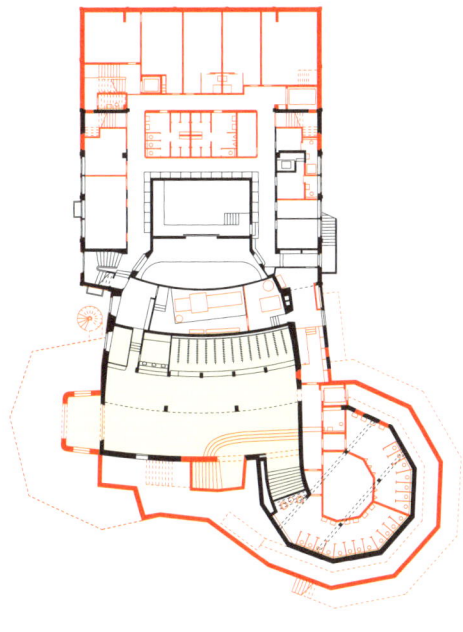

Im Nachhinein, d. h. nach der Jurierung, wurde das Weiterbauen am Sachsfoyer denkmalpflegerisch untersagt. Eine markante Projektänderung ist die Folge (2011). Im neuen, erweiterten Foyer von 1960 stecken die Knochen des alten.

Further development of the Sachsfoyer was retrospectively prohibited, i.e. after the jury decision, on grounds of monument preservation. This resulted in considerable changes to the project (2011). The bones of the old foyer of 1960 are now within the new, extended foyer.

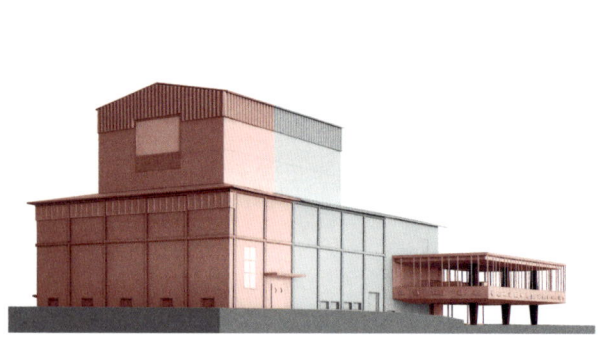
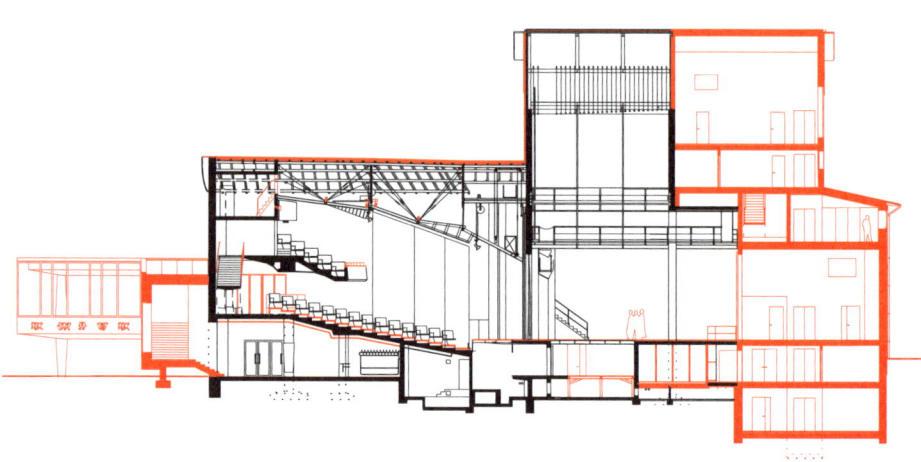
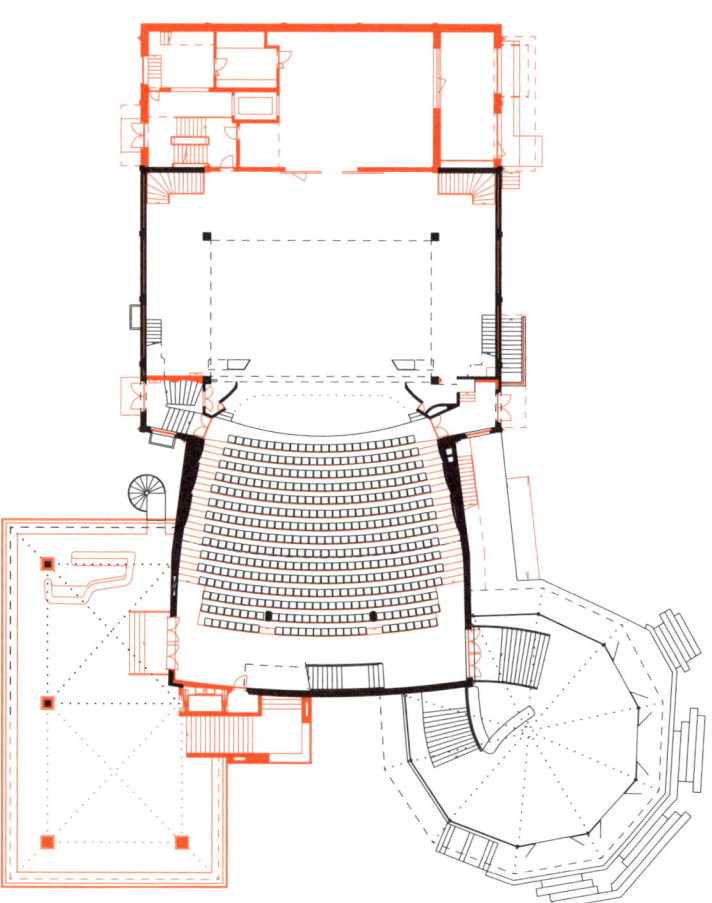
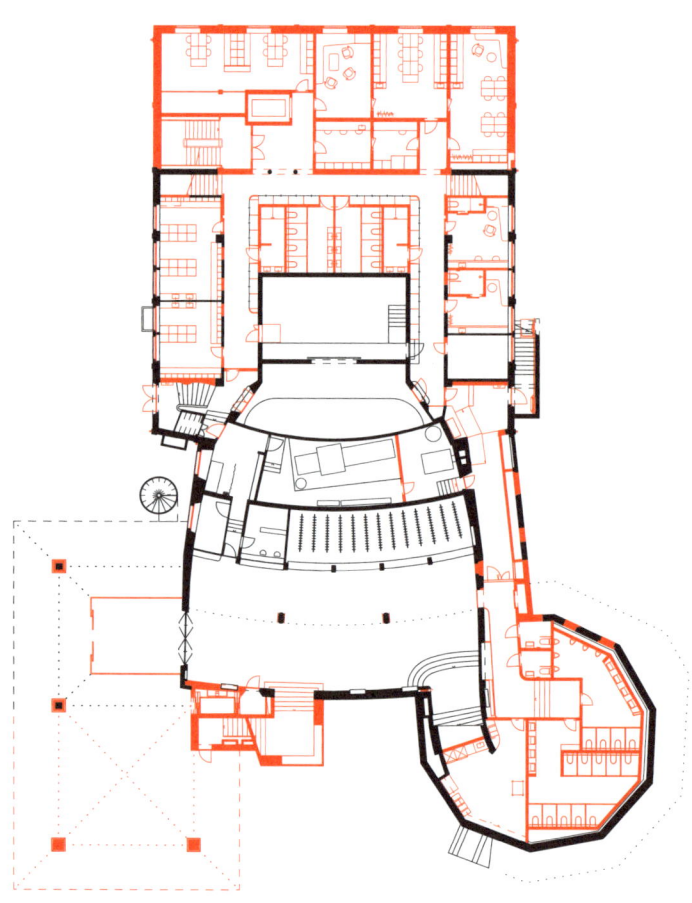

Instandsetzung und Umbau Kongresshaus/Tonhalle, Zürich

Renovation and conversion of the Kongresshaus-Tonhalle, Zurich

Baujahr / Year of construction: 1895; 1939, 1954
Architekten /Architects: Helmer & Fellner, Wien; Haefeli Moser Steiger, Zürich
Mit / With: Diener & Diener Architekten, Basel
Planerwahl / Competition: 2011
Planung und Ausführung / Planning and construction measure: 2011–2020
Bauingenieur / Civil engineer: Jürg Conzett, Chur
Aussenraumgestaltung / Landscape design: Günter Vogt, Zürich
Auftraggeber / Client: Kongresshausstiftung, Amt für Hochbauten der Stadt Zürich / Congress Hall Foundation, Canton of Zurich Construction Authority

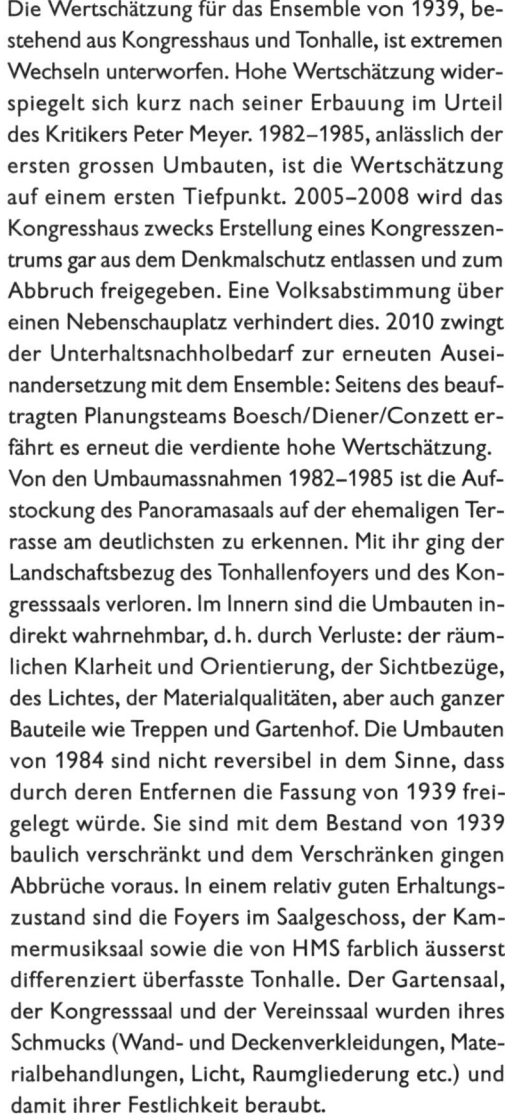

Die Wertschätzung für das Ensemble von 1939, bestehend aus Kongresshaus und Tonhalle, ist extremen Wechseln unterworfen. Hohe Wertschätzung widerspiegelt sich kurz nach seiner Erbauung im Urteil des Kritikers Peter Meyer. 1982–1985, anlässlich der ersten grossen Umbauten, ist die Wertschätzung auf einem ersten Tiefpunkt. 2005–2008 wird das Kongresshaus zwecks Erstellung eines Kongresszentrums gar aus dem Denkmalschutz entlassen und zum Abbruch freigegeben. Eine Volksabstimmung über einen Nebenschauplatz verhindert dies. 2010 zwingt der Unterhaltsnachholbedarf zur erneuten Auseinandersetzung mit dem Ensemble: Seitens des beauftragten Planungsteams Boesch/Diener/Conzett erfährt es erneut die verdiente hohe Wertschätzung.
Von den Umbaumassnahmen 1982–1985 ist die Aufstockung des Panoramasaals auf der ehemaligen Terrasse am deutlichsten zu erkennen. Mit ihr ging der Landschaftsbezug des Tonhallenfoyers und des Kongresssaals verloren. Im Innern sind die Umbauten indirekt wahrnehmbar, d. h. durch Verluste: der räumlichen Klarheit und Orientierung, der Sichtbezüge, des Lichtes, der Materialqualitäten, aber auch ganzer Bauteile wie Treppen und Gartenhof. Die Umbauten von 1984 sind nicht reversibel in dem Sinne, dass durch deren Entfernen die Fassung von 1939 freigelegt würde. Sie sind mit dem Bestand von 1939 baulich verschränkt und dem Verschränken gingen Abbrüche voraus. In einem relativ guten Erhaltungszustand sind die Foyers im Saalgeschoss, der Kammermusiksaal sowie die von HMS farblich äusserst differenziert überfasste Tonhalle. Der Gartensaal, der Kongresssaal und der Vereinssaal wurden ihres Schmucks (Wand- und Deckenverkleidungen, Materialbehandlungen, Licht, Raumgliederung etc.) und damit ihrer Festlichkeit beraubt.
Die neuen Aufgaben sind unterschiedlicher Natur (betriebliche Verbesserungen, Haustechnik, Brandschutz usw.) und sie sind mit architektonisch-städtebaulichen Intentionen zu verbinden. Der grösste derartige Eingriff, eine eigentliche Rochade, wird dort gemacht, wo das Kongresshaus nachhaltig verletzt wurde, nämlich im Bereich des Gartensaaltrakts. Mit dem Abbruch des Panoramasaals wird der Landschaftsbezug zurückgewonnen. Der Gartensaal wird zum Foyer umgewidmet und beidseitig mit zwei neuen Sälen flankiert. Ergänzend wird das heutige Restaurant im Erdgeschoss zu einer Seminarzone. Damit entsteht ein grosser zusammenhängender Kongressbereich. Gemeinsam mit dem neuen Restaurant im ersten Obergeschoss wird die einstmals beliebte Terrasse der Öffentlichkeit zurückgegeben.

Respect for the ensemble of 1939, consisting of the Kongresshaus and the Tonhalle, has varied greatly over the years. Great esteem is reflected shortly after its construction in the evaluation by the critic Peter Meyer, while conversion work between 1982 and 1985 represents the first low-point in its appreciation. Between 2005 and 2008, the Kongresshaus was even removed from the preservation list and released for demolition. However a referendum on a related issue prevented this. In 2010, the need for renovation forced the ensemble to be investigated further. The contracted planning team Boesch/Diener/Conzett, again attributes great value to the building ensemble. The conversion work between 1982 and 1985 is most apparent in the heightening of the Panoramasaal on on top of the former terrace. With it the Tonhalle foyer and Kongressaal lost their reference to the landscape. Inside, the conversion measures are indirectly evident, i.e. their negative effects: the loss of spatial clarity and orientation, visual references, light, material qualities and entire building elements such as the stairs and the garden courtyard. The conversion measures in 1984 are not reversible in the sense that their undoing would restore the building's 1939 condition. They are structurally intertwined with the 1939 building and that intervention required demolition. Only the foyers on the first upper level with their large scale sgrafitto and the Tonhalle, which received a refined colour design by HMS, a kind of "veil", remain in a relatively good condition. The Gartensaal and Kongresssaal had their decorative elements (fittings for acoustics, light and special structuring etc.) removed, thereby also depriving them of their festive character.
The new tasks are of a varied nature (functional improvements, building technology, fire protection, etc.) and they are intended to connect to architectural and urban planning intentions. The greatest such measure, which is actually a castling move, is carried out where the Kongresshaus was permanently damaged, namely in the area of the Gartensaal wing. The Panoramasaal of the 1980s is demolished to restore the relationship to the landscape. The Gartensaal is converted into a foyer and flanked on both sides by two new halls. Today's restaurant on the ground floor becomes a complementary seminar zone. These measures produce a large, connected congress area. The new restaurant on the first floor will allow the public to use the once popular terrace again.

Zustand ab / Condition after 1985

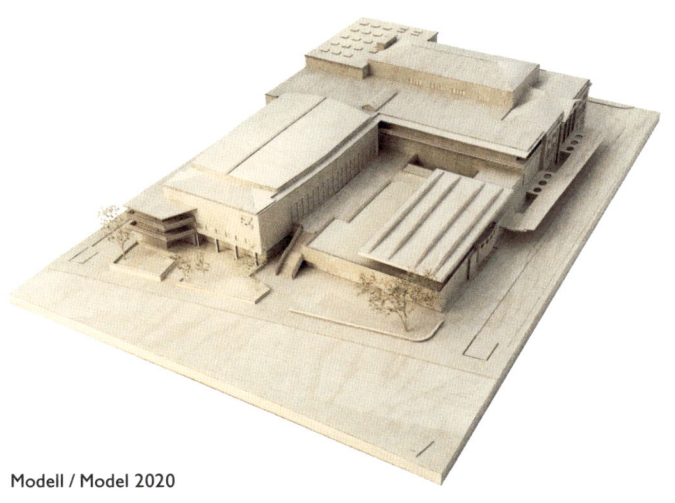

Modell / Model 2020

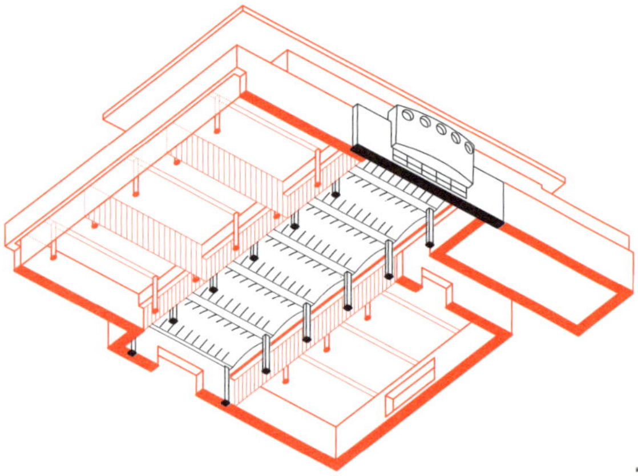

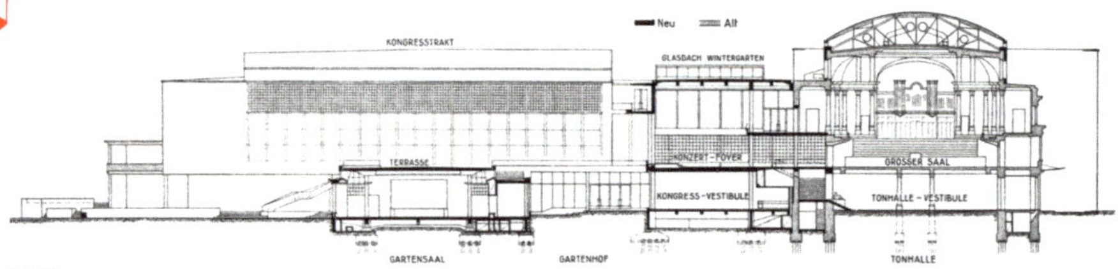

1939

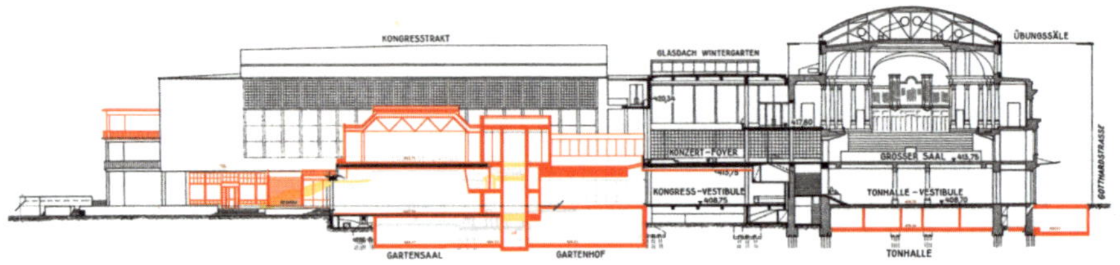

1985

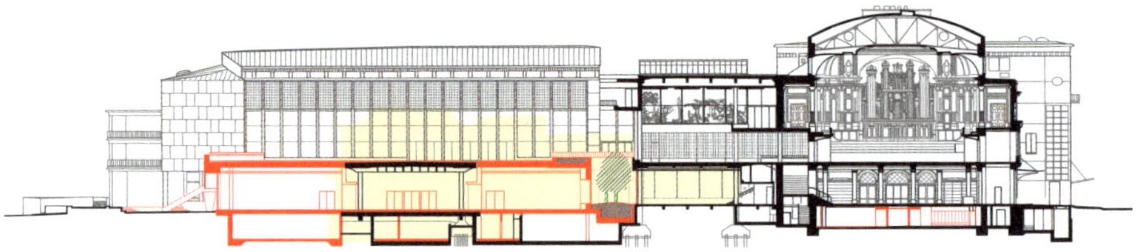

2020

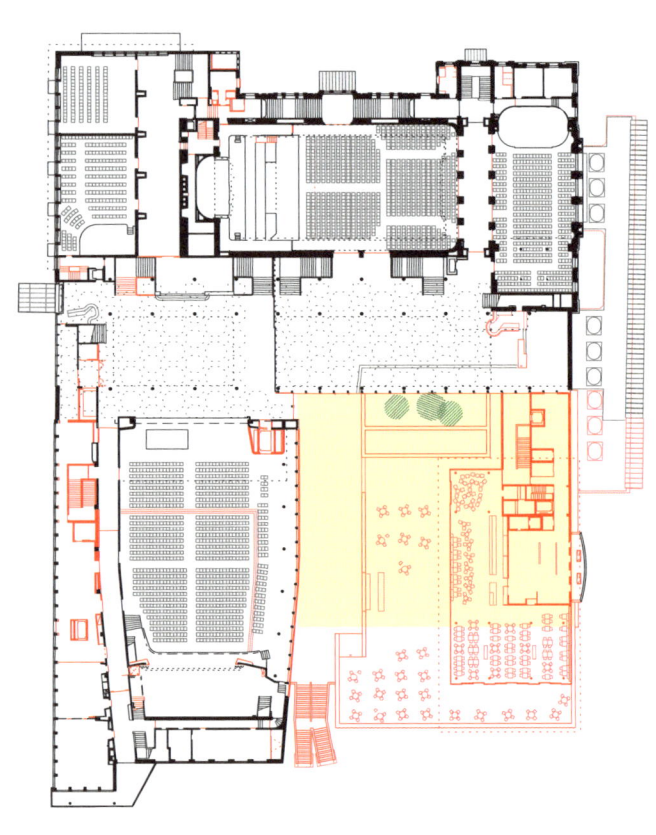

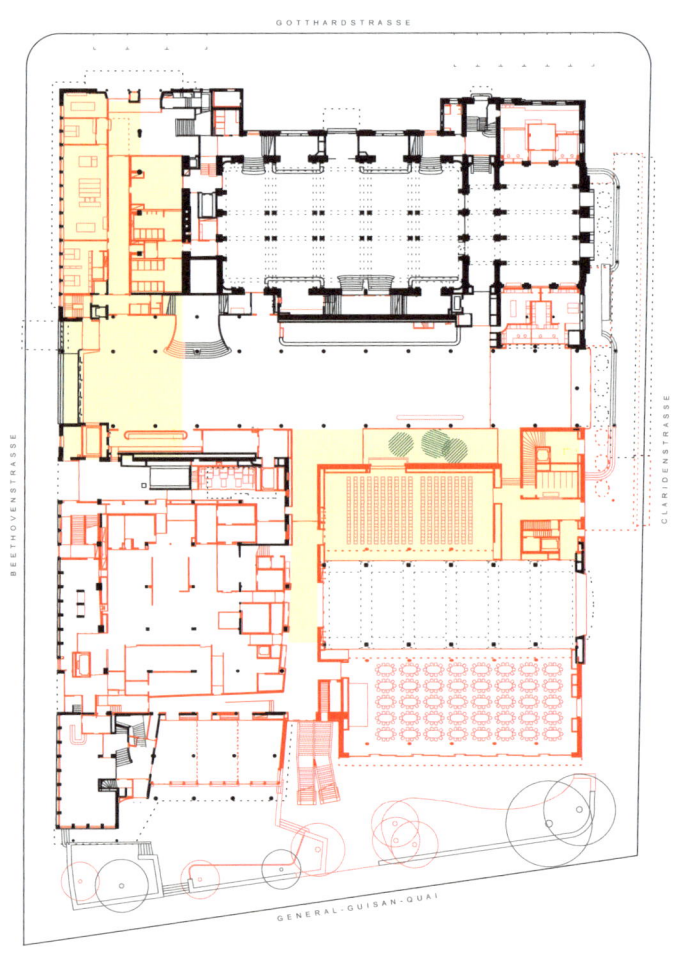

82

Sanierung Hardbrücke und fünf Aufgänge, Zürich

Hardbrücke renovation including five staircases, Zurich

Planerwahl Sanierung Hardbrücke / Competition: 2002
Direktauftrag (Aufgänge) / Direct commission (stairs): 2005
Planung und Ausführung / Planning and construction measure: 2002–2011, 2016–2017
Bauingenieur / Civil engineer: Walt + Galmarini, Zürich
Geometrie-Ingenieur / Geometry engineer: Urs B. Roth, Zürich
Auftraggeber / Client: Tiefbauamt der Stadt Zürich / City of Zurich Civil Engineering Authority

Instandsetzung eines Infrastrukturbauwerks
Die Hardbrücke, ein 1,4 km langes Infrastrukturbauwerk, weckt zwiespältige Gefühle: ein Stück Stadtautobahn und wichtige städtische Verbindung über das Gleisfeld hinweg – ein Provisorium, welches aus Sicherheitsgründen saniert werden musste. Der Wandel vom ungeliebten Grenzbauwerk zum Identifikationsobjekt und öffentlichen Raum durch die Veränderung seiner Umgebung fand innerhalb weniger Jahre statt. Aus allgemeiner Ablehnung wurde eine gewisse Zuneigung: dank der Überwindung der scharfen Trennung in Zürich-West zwischen Wohnquartieren und der ehemals «verbotenen Stadt» (die geschlossenen Industrieareale) dank der neuen Durchlässigkeit für Menschen und für neue Nutzungen.
Die baulichen Massnahmen auf, an und unter der Brücke stärken die neue Wertung. Die entwerferische Herangehensweise ist wie bei jedem anderen bestehenden Gebäude: unvoreingenommen und neugierig auf das zu entdeckende und freizulegende Potenzial, neugierig auf den (fast) immer irgendwo schlummernden Zauber einer Struktur – ob diese nun schön oder hässlich sei, gefällt oder nicht gefällt. Wie die alten so sind auch die neuen Teile hauptsächlich aus Beton. Eine Veredlung mit anderen Materialien findet nur dort statt, wo unsere Hände, unsere Füsse oder unsere Augen danach verlangen, insbesondere bei den fünf Aufgängen – z. B. Handläufe aus Holz. Die Geometrie der Aufgänge ist komplex.
Das Ansehen, die Qualität und der hohe Stellenwert des öffentlichen Raums und des öffentlichen Verkehrs in der Stadt Zürich widerspiegeln sich in der Gestaltung der sanierten Brücke und der neuen Aufgänge.

Infrastructural renovation
The Hardbrücke, an infrastructural building that is 1.4 km long, inspires mixed emotions: it is a stretch of urban motorway, an important urban connection over the railway line and a temporary solution of the 1970s that had to be renovated for reasons of safety. The transformation from an unpopular peripheral structure to an object of identification and public space as a result of changes to its surroundings has taken place within only a few years. General rejection has turned into affection, by overcoming the strict distinction in Zurich-West between residential quarters and the former "forbidden city" (closed industrial estates), in parallel with the location's new accessibility for people and new uses.
The building measures to, on and beneath the bridge strengthen its new status. The design approach to the task is the same as for any other existing building: an unprejudiced, curious attitude to the potential that can be discovered and revealed, a curiosity to find the (almost) always hidden magic of a structure – whether it is beautiful or ugly, whether pleasing or not. Like the old parts, the new sections are also mainly made of concrete. They are only refined with other materials where required by our hands, feet and eyes, especially for the five staircases – e.g. wooden railings. The geometry of the staircases is complex.
The appearance, quality and important status of the public space and public transport in the City of Zurich are reflected in the design of the renovated bridge and the new staircases.

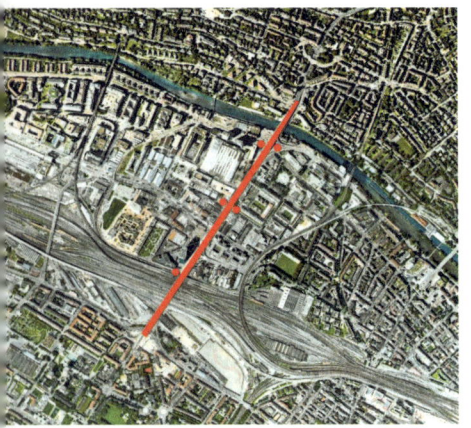

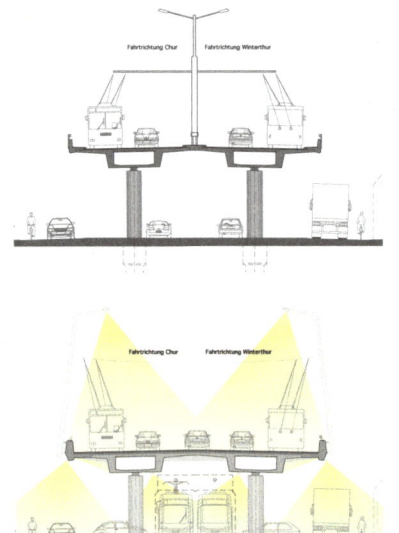

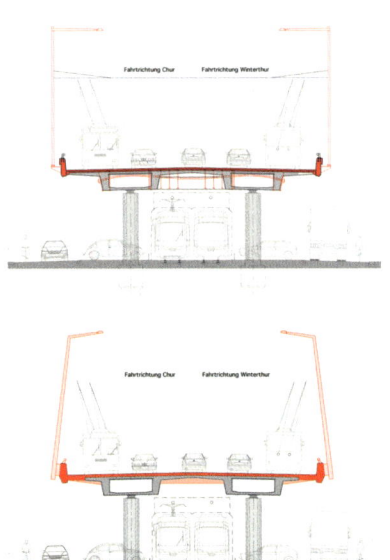

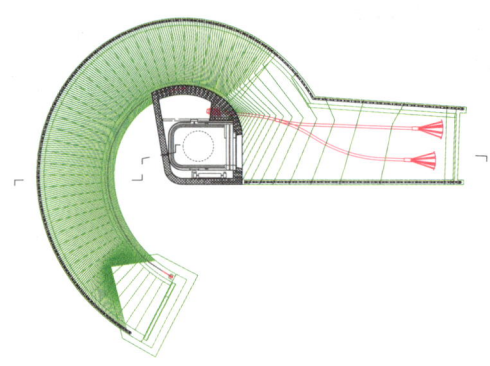

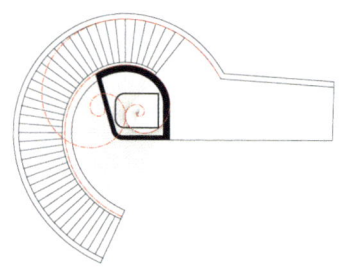
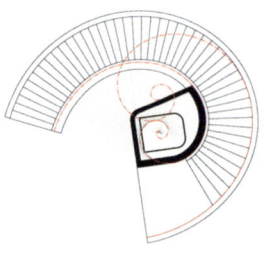

88

Werkverzeichnis / List of works
Auswahl Bauten, Projekte und Wettbewerbe / Selection of Buildings, Projects and Competitions

1982–1984		Um- und Anbau Haus B-T, Feldmeilen
1985–1991		Umbauten in Berlin, Tokio, Hongkong etc. für Jil Sander
1986		Praxis Dr. F, Wil; Um- und Ausbau
1987	1	Wettbewerb Gemeinschaftszentrum, Igis-Landquart
1988		Praxis Dr. F, Baden; Um- und Ausbau
1989		Praxis Dr. A, Zürich; Um- und Ausbau
		J. S. Lamp
1989–1990		Drei Umbauten, Basel, Lausanne
1990	2	J. S. Bench
		Projekt, Harrods, London; Ausbau
1991		Projekt, Wohnhaus, Berneck; Anbau
1992		Studienauftrag Bankgebäude SKA, St. Gallen; Um- und Ausbau
1991–1993	3	Geschäftshaus, Zürich; Neuausbau
1992–1993		Boutique Akris, Imperial Plaza Hotel, Tokio; Ausbau
1993		Ausstellungsgestaltung «Fukuoka»; mit Vito Bertin im Architektur Forum Zürich
	4	«Feindbild Hochhaus», Beitrag zur Ausstellung im Architektur Forum Zürich
1993–1994	5	Projekt, Galerie für antike fernöstliche Kunst, Zürich; Umbau
1994	6	E-Tischli «Moser/Bill/Boesch»
		Haus A, Küsnacht; Instandsetzung
		Praxis Dr. Z, Zürich; Um- und Ausbau
		Wettbewerb EWA Elektrizitätswerke Altdorf
1995		Wettbewerb Areal Feldbach, Steckborn
1994–1995		Haus F, Wil; Um- und Ausbau
1993–1996	7	Hochhaus zur Palme (1956–1964, Haefeli Moser Steiger), Zürich; Um- und Ausbau
1996		Studienauftrag Erneuerung Shopville, Zürich
	8	Studienauftrag ETH-Hauptgebäude, Zürich (Gottfried Semper/Gustav Gull)
1997	9	Studienauftrag Erweiterung Altersheim, Berneck
		Wettbewerb Begegnungszentrum, psychiatrische Klinik, Königsfelden

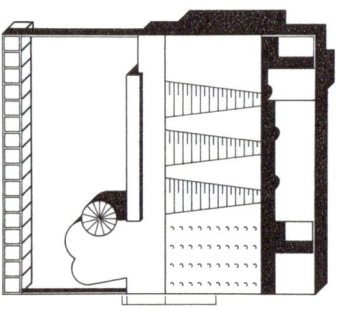

1

2

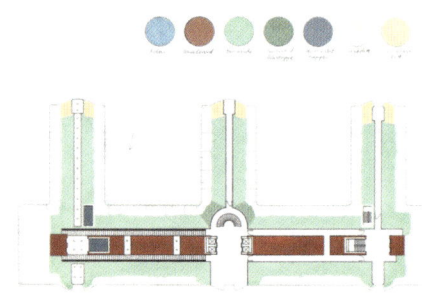

3

4

5

6

1994–1997		Praxis Dr. A, Frauenfeld; Um- und Ausbau
1998	10	Ausstellungsgestaltung im Deutsches Architektur Museum Frankfurt am Main (1984, O. M. Ungers); mit Martin Tschanz
1999		Haus E, Oberstammheim; Umbau
	11	Wettbewerb Gesamtschule, Volketswil
		Wettbewerb Stadtsaal, Baden
2001		Städtebauliche Studie, Wollerau; mit Thomas Schregenberger
2000–2001	12	Studienauftrag Jugendherberge, Zürich (1969–1966, Ernst Gisel); Umbau, Teilersatz
1997–2001		Roche Basel, Bau 74 (1974, Roland Rohn); Ausbau
2002		Studienauftrag Wohnungsbau Behinda, Zürich-Schwamendingen
		Studienauftrag Restaurant EPI-Klinik (1971, Bruno Giacometti), Zürich
2001–2002		Pavillon Oui!, expo.02, Yverdon-les-Bains
2003		Ausstellungsgestaltung «Gartenlust», Architektur Forum Zürich
2002–2003	13	Studienauftrag Geschenk der Schweiz an die UNO, New York
		Studie Tiefencastel
2003–2004		Wohnhaus S-M, Zürich
2005		Wettbewerb Kindergarten, Mollis
1997–2005		Instandsetzung Verwaltungsgebäude, Niederurnen
2003–2005		Umbau Werkhof Uraniastrasse, Zürich (1914, Gustav Gull)
2004–2005		Studienauftrag Villa Rämistrasse 66 (1863, vermutlich Leonhard Zeugheer), Zürich
2006		Städtebauliche Studie Murtenstrasse, Bern
2000–2006		Studienauftrag und Sonderbauvorschriften Maag-Areal, Zürich; mit Diener & Diener, Basel
2007	14	Studienauftrag Villa Patumbah (1883–1885, Alfred Chiodera, Theophil Tschudy), Zürich
		Machbarkeitsstudie ZHAW Sulzerareal, Winterthur; Erweiterung
		Städtebauliche Studie Lagerplatz (Sulzerareal), Winterthur
2005–2008		Um- und Anbau Villa Rainhof, Zürich

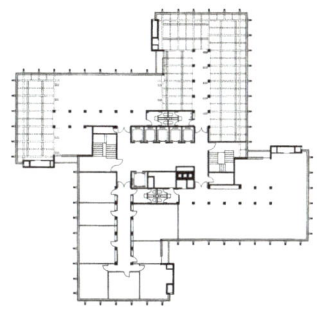

7

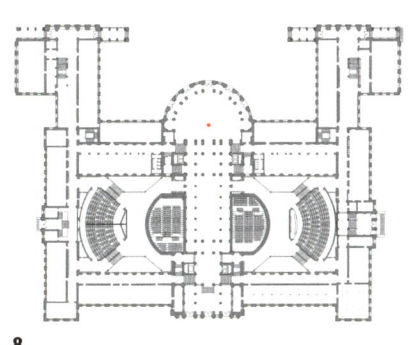

8

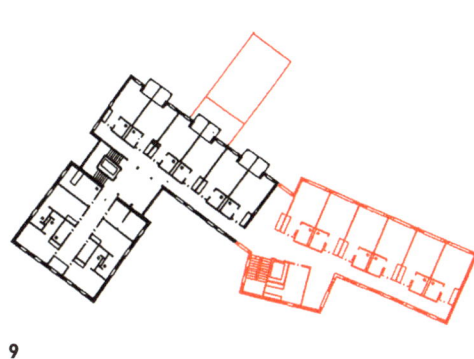

9

10

11

12

2006–2008		Gartenhalle, Gartenhaus, Berneck
		Instandsetzung Haus Kind, Riehen (1930, Bräuning Leu)
2009	15	Studienauftrag Tonhalle, St. Gallen (1909, G. J. Kunkler/Robert Maillart)
		Wettbewerb Max-Frisch-Platz, Zürich; mit Hager Landschaftsarchitekten
		Studienauftrag Sockelmauer Kirche St. Mauritius, Appenzell
		Umbau und Erweiterung Musikinsel Kloster Rheinau
2010		Studienauftrag Weinhaus, Wilchingen
	16	Testplanung, Stadt Zürich AfS, Seeufergestaltung Quaianlagen
		Studienauftrag Historisches und Völkerkundemuseum, St. Gallen
2011		Studie Haus K, Zürich; Umbau und Erweiterung
		Studienauftrag Theater Oxer, Umbau Reithalle, Aarau
1997–2011		Umbau und Instandsetzung Amtshaus III, Zürich (1914, Gustav Gull)
2012		Studienauftrag Erweiterung Schulhaus und neue Turnhalle, Rikon
	17	Studie Umbau und Restaurierung dreier Altstadthäuser, Zug
2011–2012		Studienauftrag Städtebauliche Studie Tour Henri, Fribourg
2013	18	Wohnung (2013 Meili Peter Architekten), Zürich; Umbau
2012–2013		Studie Villa Sträuli, Winterthur
		Studienauftrag Revitalisierung Kloster Kappel, Kappel am Albis
		Studie Haus B, Zürich
2014		Wettbewerb Kindergarten, Heerbrugg
		Wettbewerb Turnhalle, Yverdon
2002–2017		Sanierung Hardbrücke und fünf Aufgänge, Zürich
2018		Installation *Riuso/reuse* Architektur-Biennale, 2018, Venedig

Laufende Projekte

2007–2020	Instandsetzung, Umbau und Erweiterung, Kurtheater, Baden (1952, Lisbeth Sachs/Otto Dorer Architekten; Studienauftrag 2007, 1. Preis)
2011–2020	Instandsetzung und Umbau Kongresshaus/Tonhalle, Zürich; Diener & Diener, Basel (1895, Helmer & Fellner, Wien; 1939, Haefeli Moser Steiger, Zürich; Wettbewerb 2011)

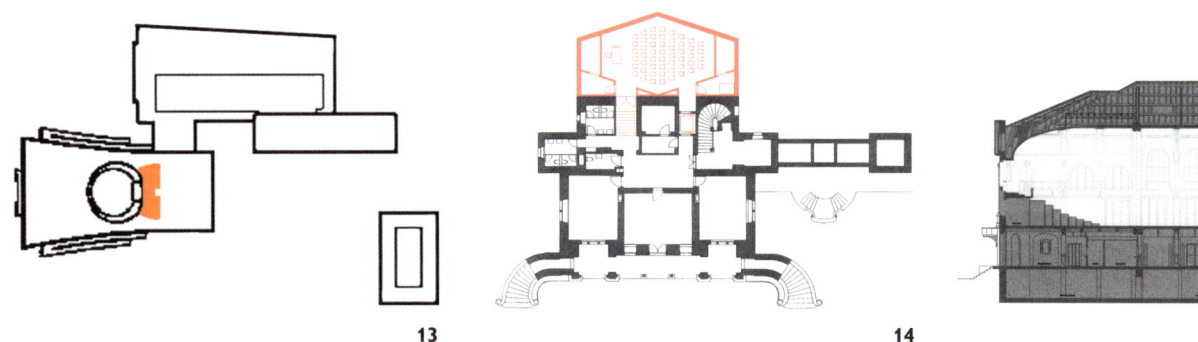

13 14 15

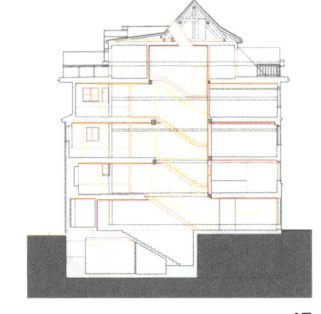
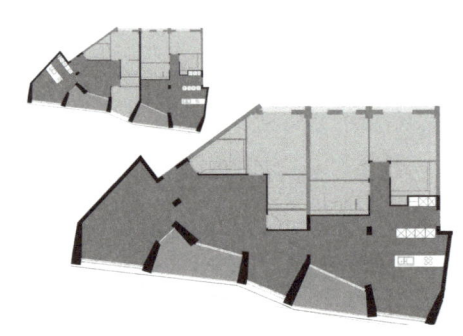

16 17 18

Elisabeth Boesch

	1951	geboren in Berneck SG
	1976	Architekturdiplom an der ETH Zürich bei Prof. Dolf Schnebli
	1976–1981	Mitarbeit bei Mario Botta, Lugano und Fribourg
	1983–	gemeinsames Architekturbüro in Zürich mit Martin Boesch
	1993–2005	Vorstandsmitglied im Architektur Forum Zürich
	1995	Mitglied BSA
	1995	EPFL Lausanne, professeur invité zusammen mit Martin Boesch
	2000–2011	Mitglied im Zentralvorstand des BSA (Bund Schweizer Architekten) und Initiantin des BSA-Forschungsstipendiums
	2007	ZHAW, Winterthur, Gastdozentur
	2002–	Mitglied verschiedener Stadtbildkommissionen (Altdorf, Baden, Wetzikon, Opfikon, Schlieren)
	2003–	Mitglied der Natur- und Heimatschutzkommission NHK des Kantons Zürich
	1951	Born in Berneck SG
	1976	Graduated in Architecture at the ETH Zurich under Prof. Dolf Schnebli
	1976–1981	Employment at Mario Botta, Lugano and Fribourg
	1983–	Joint architectural office in Zurich with Martin Boesch
	1993–2005	Committee Member, Architektur Forum Zürich
	1995	Member of the BSA (Federation of Swiss Architects)
	1995	Guest Professor at the EPFL Lausanne with Martin Boesch
	2000–2011	Central Committee Member of the BSA and initiator of the BSA Research Scholarship
	2007	Guest Lecturer at the ZHAW Winterthur
	2002–	Member of various town planning committees (Altdorf, Baden, Wetzikon, Opfikon, Schlieren)
	2003–	Member of the Natur- und Heimatschutzkommission (NHK), Canton of Zurich

Martin Boesch

	1951	geboren in Zürich
	1978	Architekturdiplom an der ETH Zürich bei Prof. Dolf Schnebli
	1975–1983	Praktikum und Mitarbeit bei Mario Botta, Lugano, und Ernst Gisel, Zürich
	1983–	gemeinsames Architekturbüro in Zürich mit Elisabeth Boesch
	1995	Mitglied BSA
	1995	EPFL Lausanne, professeur invité zusammen mit Elisabeth Boesch
	1998–	Mitglied der Heinrich Tessenow-Gesellschaft und Heinrich Tessenow-Stiftung, Hamburg. Forschungen zu Heinrich Tessenow
	1999–2002	Hochschule für bildende Künste Hamburg, ETH-Zürich, Gastdozentur
	1997–2007	Institut d'Architecture Université de Genève IAUG, Gastprofessur
	2009–2011	HafenCity Universität Hamburg HCU, Sutor-Stiftungsprofessur
	2011–2012	ZHAW, Winterthur, Gastdozentur
	2005–	Accademia di architettura Mendrisio USI AAM, Titular-Professur
	2010–2017	Mitglied der Wakker-Kommission
	1951	Born in Zurich
	1978	Graduated in Architecture at the ETH Zurich under Prof. Dolf Schnebli
	1975–1983	Internship and employment at Mario Botta, Lugano and Ernst Gisel
	1983–	Joint architectural office in Zurich with Elisabeth Boesch
	1995	Member of the BSA (Federation of Swiss Architects)
	1995	Guest Professor at the EPFL Lausanne with Elisabeth Boesch
	1998–	Member of the Heinrich Tessenow Society and the Heinrich Tessenow Foundation, Hamburg. Research on Heinrich Tessenow
	1999–2002	Guest Lecturer, Hochschule für bildende Künste HfbK Hamburg and the ETH Zurich
	1997–2007	Guest Professor, Institut d'Architecture Université de Genève IAUG
	2009–2011	Sutor Foundation Professor, HafenCity Universität Hamburg HCU
	2011–2012	Guest Lecturer, ZHAW Winterthur
	2005–	Titular Professor, Accademia di architettura Mendrisio USI AAM
	2010–2017	Member of the Wakker Commission

MitarbeiterInnen / Collaborators   Silvio Albin , Thijs ten Brummelhuis, Liesa Fischer, Cristina Fusco, Gaia Pelizzari, Henri Vázquez Dietiker, Elias Vollmeier

Nils Krämer, Laetitia Bernasconi, Gordian Blumenthal, Jonathan Bopp, David Brunner, Silvio Bühlmann, Elettra Carnelli, Federica Eichelberg, Ole Drescher, Alice Fakhri, Jérôme Haefeli, Jules Hausherr, Johanna Hofmeister, Philippe Jorisch, Myra Kamber, Fabian Kiepenheuer, Alain Kilchenmann, Sebastian Krieg, Konrad Mäder, Sophie Maffioli, Michael Meier, Stéphanie Morel, Shotaro Morikawa, Davide Pellegrino, André Perronnet, Ulrike Puchta, Ivo Raffi, Christoph Ramser, Julia Remane, Petra Ring, Fabian Roth, Marceline Ruckstuhl, Dorothea Schmidt, Elia Schneider, Christina Schnitzler, Fabian Singler, Stephan Sintzel, Chris Stepan, Monika Stöckli, Alexander Sumic, Oliver Suter, Philipp Ullrich, Santina Di Vincenzo, Anna Walewska, Nina Lund Westerdahl, Reto Wasser, Rainer Weitschies, Sonja Widmer, Claudia Wintsch, Andreas Wipf, Bianca Zucchi

Finanzielle und ideelle Unterstützung
Financial and conceptual support

Ein besonderer Dank gilt den Institutionen und Sponsorfirmen, deren finanzielle Unterstützungen wesentlich zum Entstehen dieser Buchreihe beitragen.
Ihr kulturelles Engagement ermöglicht ein fruchtbares und freundschaftliches Zusammenwirken von Baukultur und Bauwirtschaft.

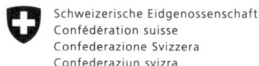

Ein besonderer Dank für die Unterstützung dieses Buchprojektes geht an Frau B. S. in Zürich

EMCH Aufzüge AG, Bern

Gruenberg + Partner AG, Zürich

Urs Mätzler Schreinerei, Berneck

Quart Verlag Luzern / Quart Editions Lucerne

De aedibus – Zeitgenössische Architekten und ihre Bauten / Contemporary architects and their buildings

74	Elisabeth & Martin Boesch (de/en)	37	Althammer Hochuli (de/en)
73	spaceshop Architekten (de/en)	36	Schneider & Schneider (de/en)
72	Kast Kaeppeli (de/en)	35	Frei & Ehrensperger (de und en)
71	Philippe Meyer (de/en/fr)	34	Liechti Graf Zumsteg (de/en)
70	bartbuchhofer (de/en)	33	Adrian Streich (de/en)
69	Hauenstein La Roche Schedler (de/en)	32	Daniele Marques (de/en)
68	Graeme Mann & Patricia Capua Mann (de/en)	31	Neff Neumann (de/en)
67	Esposito Javet (de/en und de/fr)	30	Giraudi Wettstein (de/en)
66	Galletti Matter (de/en und de/fr)	29	Steinmann & Schmid (de/en)
65	Fruehauf, Henry & Viladoms (de/en)	28	Matthias Ackermann (de/en)
64	Jakob Steib (de/en)	27	Aeby & Perneger (de/en)
63	bunq (de/en)	26	Bakker & Blanc (de/en)
62	Jean-Paul Jaccaud (de/en und de/fr)	25	Markus Wespi Jérôme de Meuron (de/en)
61	huggenbergerfries (de/en)	24	Bauart (de/en und de/fr)
60	Berrel Berrel Kräutler (de/en)	23	Knapkiewicz & Fickert (de/en)
59	Pierre-Alain Dupraz (de/en und de/fr)	22	Marcel Ferrier (de/en)
58	Cometti Truffer (de/en)	21	Wild Bär Architekten (de/en)
57	Joos & Mathys (de/en)	20	Enzmann + Fischer (de/en)
56	Lacroix Chessex (de/en)	19	Mierta und Kurt Lazzarini (de/en)
55	Savioz Fabrizzi (de/en und de/fr)	18	Rolf Mühlethaler (de/en)
54	Boegli Kramp (de/en)	17	Pablo Horváth (de/en)
53	Zita Cotti (de/en)	16	Brauen + Wälchli (de/en)
52	Oestreich + Schmid (de/en)	15	E2A Eckert Eckert Architekten (de/en)
51	Stump & Schibli Architekten (de/en)	14	Lussi + Halter (de/en)
50	Luca Gazzaniga (de/en)	13	Philipp Brühwiler (de/en)
49	Guignard & Saner (de/en)	12	Scheitlin – Syfrig + Partner (de/en)
48	Morger + Dettli (de/en)	11	Vittorio Magnago Lampugnani (de/en)
47	Charles Pictet (de/en)	10	Bonnard Woeffray (de/en und de/fr)
46	Armando Ruinelli + Partner (de/en/it)	9	Graber Pulver (de/en)
45	Luca Selva Architekten (de/en)	8	Burkhalter Sumi/Makiol Wiederkehr (de/en)
44	Luca Deon (de/en)	7	Gigon/Guyer (de und en)
43	2b (de/en)	6	Andrea Bassi (de, fr und en)
42	Durisch + Nolli (de/en)	5	Dieter Jüngling und Andreas Hagmann (de und en)
41	sabarchitekten (de/en)	4	Beat Consoni (de und en)
40	Beat Rothen (de/en)	3	Max Bosshard & Christoph Luchsinger (de)
39	Atelier Bonnet (de/en)	2	Miroslav Šik (de, en und it)
38	Novaron (de/en)	1	Valentin Bearth & Andrea Deplazes (de, en und it)

Quart Verlag GmbH, Heinz Wirz; Verlag für Architektur und Kunst
Denkmalstrasse 2, CH-6006 Luzern; books@quart.ch, www.quart.ch